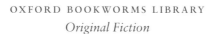

OXFORD BOOKWORMS LIBRARY
Original Fiction

Not Without You

GILL HARVEY

Stage 5 (1800 headwords)

T0347603

Illustrated by Paul McCaffrey

Series Editor: Rachel Bladon
Founder Editors: Jennifer Bassett
and Tricia Hedge

OXFORD
UNIVERSITY PRESS

Great Clarendon Street, Oxford, OX2 6DP, United Kingdom

Oxford University Press is a department of the University of Oxford.
It furthers the University's objective of excellence in research, scholarship,
and education by publishing worldwide. Oxford is a registered trade
mark of Oxford University Press in the UK and in certain other countries

ISBN: 978 0 19 463435 9   Book

A complete recording of this Bookworms edition of *Not Without You* is available.

Printed in China

Word count (main text): 22,815

For more information on the Oxford Bookworms Library,
visit www.oup.com/elt/gradedreaders

ACKNOWLEDGEMENTS

Cover by: Paul McCaffrey/Sylvie Poggio Artists.

Illustrations by: Paul McCaffrey/Sylvie Poggio Artists.

The publisher would like to thank the following for permission to reproduce photographs:
Alamy Stock Photo p.97 (flight simulator/001 Images).

CONTENTS

Foreword   1

1 One Year Together   2
2 The Fruit of the Wild Rose   9
3 Pod Life   16
4 Cham's Idea   23
5 Swimming with Dolphins   27
6 Sala's Decision   34
7 A Difficult Choice   40
8 Passenger Cham   47
9 Wena   54
10 Sala's News   60
11 Ultranet Talk Hour   66
12 Looking for Answers   72
13 Not the Same Person   78
14 Contact Hour   84
15 Coming In   91

GLOSSARY   94
BEYOND THE STORY   97
ACTIVITIES: Think Ahead   99
ACTIVITIES: Chapter Check   100
ACTIVITIES: Focus on Vocabulary   104
ACTIVITIES: Focus on Language   105
ACTIVITIES: Discussion   106
PROJECT   107
RECOMMENDED READING   109

Foreword

It is 2088, thirty years since the end of the ten-year Oil Wars. Sala and Cham live in an enormous overcrowded city that they are forbidden to leave, for their own protection: the world outside the city was contaminated during the wars.

Because the Oil Wars left the city short of energy, everyone has a small chip buried under the skin on their wrists, which measures how many units of energy they use. It also notes where they are at all times, to keep them safe.

The government uses most of the city's energy to build virtual simulations, so that people can experience beautiful places without actually going anywhere. They cannot travel, but there will be no more wars. The city is at peace.

1

One Year Together

Sala and her friend Niki pushed past the people who had gathered in the rain outside the meat-growing laboratory. They were all shouting angrily, "Work! We want work!"

Government agents had just arrived, so the crowd would soon be forced to leave. Sala was so busy staring that she didn't look where she was going, and stepped into water up to her ankles.

"Urgh!" she said. Her right boot was wet through. "Let's get out of here."

"What was that about?" asked Niki, as they hurried on down the street. "What are they all doing there?"

"My mom says the packing equipment is broken," said Sala. Her mom was a scientist in the laboratory. "So they're demanding the packing work instead."

"And will they get it?" asked Niki.

Sala shook her head. "Mom says the equipment will soon be fixed. Anyway, there are loads of robots doing the work for now."

"So they're just getting wet for no reason?" said Niki. "What a life! Too many people, no jobs, and rain, rain, rain."

"Yeah," agreed Sala.

It was true; life for most people *was* difficult. But actually, Sala was feeling really happy. It was March 15, and she had been going out with Cham for exactly one year. She could say with her hand on her heart that this year – her eighteenth – had been the best so far. Absolutely. The. Best.

They reached the simulator center, and Sala lifted her wrist to touch a gray screen by the door. The little chip under her skin lit up for a second, showing how many energy units she had left. Everyone was given one hundred energy units a week, and they had to be careful not to use them too quickly. A simulator cost five units per hour, which was a lot – but it was worth it for the escape it offered from the city.

Inside, Niki went to meet some other friends while Sala looked around the busy entrance area for Cham. When she saw him over by the taste-pot machine, her heart jumped. It was crazy the way it did that, even after a whole year together.

"Hey," said Cham, as she joined him. He smiled and kissed her, then gave her a taste-pot with a spoon: "I got your favorite. Double chocolate."

"Aww... that's so sweet of you!" Taste-pots were great, because they weren't expensive, but gave you the taste of something luxurious like double chocolate ice cream. There were hundreds of tastes to choose from.

"We have Space 234. Maybe we could go to the beach?"

Sala nodded. "Perfect."

At Space 234, they stepped inside the little room and closed the door. At once, there was silence: the noise of all the people outside was completely shut out. There was a screen on the wall with a list of places to choose from: places they would never see for real.

Sala chose the *Beach* illusion, and the walls of the room disappeared. Instead, there was calm blue ocean as far as they could see, under a cloudless sky. Sunlight shone through the trees above, and soft golden sand seemed to lie at their feet. All they could hear were the sounds of the waves and the gentle wind in the trees. It was a really wonderful illusion.

"Fantastic," said Sala, taking off her wet boots. "I love this simulation."

They sat down to eat their taste-pots, looking out at the beautiful view and watching the waves roll up the shore. Then, after her final spoonful, Sala reached for her bag.

"I have something for you. A present."

She gave Cham a package, then sat watching his expression as he slowly opened it.

"Hey!" said Cham. "It's one of your paintings!"

"Yes." Sala loved painting, but the paints were expensive, so it was something she couldn't do very often.

"Wow!" Cham studied it.

"You like it?"

"I love it," said Cham. "It's you and me, right? And a waterfall behind us." He smiled. "Not *a* waterfall. *The* waterfall."

Sala nodded. "To remind you of the day we met."

"You think I'd forget?" he laughed. "Not a chance."

Sala would never forget, either. One year ago, on March 15, 2087, she'd been standing in Space 29 in one of her favorite illusions. She was on the top of a cliff looking down at a valley, with fields and forests that went on and on. On the other side of the valley, the white waters of a waterfall flowed over the rocks. It was one of the best illusions available in the simulator, because if you stood at the edge of the cliff, it really felt like you could fall.

And then someone had opened the door, making the whole illusion break up. Sala had been so surprised she'd almost screamed. She'd turned around quickly and seen a boy: about her age but a little taller, with black hair and dark, smiling eyes… Sala had stared. He was gorgeous.

"Oops, sorry!" he'd said. "Wrong space!"

Sala had stared.
He was gorgeous.

"Oh! That's OK," Sala had replied quickly. "You can stay here if you want."

She didn't know where those words had come from. Usually, she was shy with boys. But Cham had come in and closed the door, and they had started to talk. Sala had soon found out that he lived near her, in an earth apartment. He loved the same ultranet games and story-streams as her, and the same illusions in the simulator. Best of all, he made her laugh. By the time they left the simulator, she'd fallen in love – and luckily for her, so had Cham.

Cham put the painting down. "I have something for you, too."

"Another double choc taste-pot?"

"Nope." Cham smiled, his eyes shining. "Try again."

Sala had no idea. "A diamond necklace?" she joked.

"In your dreams!"

"Cham!" Sala giggled. "Don't make me guess!"

"OK, OK," laughed Cham. "Take a look at your ultranet."

Sala looked at Cham, and engaged her virtual interface.

"Go on," Cham encouraged her.

Sala looked up at her interface. The letters *PA* appeared, followed by the face of a young woman.

"*Hello, Sala. This is Pod Adventures*," said the woman, in a friendly voice.

Sala's mouth dropped open. A pod experience?

"*Sala, you and Cham are going to swim with dolphins.*"

"No!" cried Sala. She stared at Cham. "Really?"

She couldn't believe it. A pod was like a simulator, but a million times better. Your whole body lay inside the pod and it was like your normal life was turned off. In a simulator, it was hard to forget that there were four walls just five or six steps away – but in a pod, you lost your awareness of the world around you. You lived the experience completely.

Cham smiled at her. "Happy?"

"*Yes!*" Sala had never had a pod experience. They were expensive. She didn't know how Cham could afford it, but he was always so kind and generous – it would be rude to ask. She wrapped her arms around him and buried her face in his neck. "Thank you, thank you. You're the best! I love you so much."

The hour on the beach was soon over. Sala and Cham left, and met three friends in another space – Niki, and two boys named Palo and Ding. With five of them sharing, an hour cost just one energy unit each, so they did this often. For the first thirty minutes, they chose the illusion of a big nightclub with a famous band playing. Then they changed to a sunny park, like the ones that their city used to have, and sat down to talk.

"Guess what," said Ding. "I heard the government has a new idea – about people living in pods."

"Oh yeah," said Palo. "Pod Life. I saw something about it, too. But it's not just an idea. It's happening. It's starting really soon – in a couple of weeks, I think."

Sala was curious. "I haven't heard anything," she said. "What's it all about?"

"It's like a pod experience, but you stay in for much longer," explained Ding. "They've developed these special pods that you can actually live in. They connect your body to them and look after it for you – your food, your muscles, everything. So you don't need to move. You live there. Inside the pod."

"*Live* there!" gasped Sala. It was one thing to have a pod experience – but to stay inside the pod was something else. "For how long?"

"I think they're saying two years, at least," said Palo.

Sala's mouth dropped open. "But who would want to do that?"

"People who want to earn money and energy units," said Ding. "They give you both while you're in there. And you get to study, I think."

"Yeah. They've designed special study programs," explained Palo.

Sala frowned. "But we already study virtually most of the time."

"This is at another level, I guess. They're saying that the study programs in the pod will make you much more employable when you come out."

"And they actually *pay* you?" Niki's eyes were wide.

"Yes," said Palo. "They really want people to do it. It will save space and energy, they say."

"Oooh, strange!" said Niki. "But interesting, too."

"I'd hate it," said Sala. "Can you imagine?" She looked across at Cham. He was quiet, just listening. It was unusual for him. "Living in a pod. Urgh!"

"You sound like your grandmother," joked Ding.

Sala laughed. "Maybe."

Actually, Ding was probably right. Sala's grandmother remembered life before the Oil Wars, when people could travel freely and see other parts of the world. Now Gran believed in encouraging people to enjoy the real world, instead of constantly escaping to the simulators or the ultranet. She'd made her own garden on the roof of their apartment, and she was always up there. The rest of her family jokingly called it her "Real Space."

2

The Fruit of the Wild Rose

When Sala and Cham left the simulator center, it was dark, and still raining. To get home quickly, they stepped onto one of the fast-moving walkways that stretched in all directions across the city.

As they traveled, towering blocks of apartments rose up high all around them. Most of them had at least forty floors above ground – these were called "sky apartments." Below ground, there were often another ten floors, for "earth apartments." The government had started building under the ground long ago, because the land inside the city was so limited.

Sala and Cham stepped off the walkway near their apartment blocks, and as they did so, someone knocked Sala's elbow, then held her arm for a second.

Sala turned quickly: a young woman stood there. She was maybe a year or two older than Sala and Cham. She had a hat pulled low over her face, so it was partly hidden, but Sala could just see her green eyes.

The woman reached for Sala's hand and slipped a small package into it. "Give this to your grandmother," she said, and then turned away.

Sala's mouth dropped open. "Sorry? What... Wait!"

But she was too late. The woman had already jumped back onto the speeding walkway. It carried her away rapidly, and in no time at all, she'd disappeared.

"Who was that?" asked Cham.

"No idea." Sala stared down at the little package in her hand. It was made of clear plastic, and inside, there was some kind of small dark red fruit. It looked old and dry. Sala frowned. She'd never seen anything like it before.

"Must be something for Gran's garden," she said.

"Yeah, that makes sense," Cham agreed. "Well, I guess I'd better go. Mom's expecting me."

Sala put her arms around him and kissed him.

"Thank you so much, again," she said. "I've had a great time, and I can't *wait* to go swimming with dolphins."

"Good," said Cham. "And thanks for my painting, too. I love it." But his voice sounded strange… distant, almost.

Sala frowned. She remembered how quiet he'd been with their friends. Usually, Cham had plenty to say, and loved making everyone laugh.

"Cham, is everything OK?" she asked.

"Yes, yes," he said. "Why?"

"You seem worried about something."

Cham seemed to hesitate.

"Is it your dad?" Sala asked. "Is he looking for work again?"

Cham smiled, and shook his head. "No, he's helping fix the equipment at the meat-growing laboratory, actually, and getting reasonable money for it. Honestly, it's nothing. I'll see you on the ultranet later, OK?"

"You're sure?"

"Sure."

They'd been standing under one of the shelters at the entrance to the walkway. Cham kissed her, and before Sala could say anything else, he turned and ran out into the rain.

Sala watched him go, puzzled. *It's nothing*, he'd said. She wished she could believe him. But it was odd. All at once, she was sure that something wasn't right.

She turned and ran down the street to her apartment block,

and soon she was in the dry and rushing upward in the elevator. Twenty… twenty-five… the floors passed by so quickly. With a loud *beep*, the doors opened at floor sixty-three: the top. Sala walked out, and the screen on the door of her apartment recognized her, and let her in.

"Is that you, Sala?" called a voice from somewhere above.

"Yes, Gran. Are you in the Real Space?"

"Of course," called Gran. "Come on up!"

Sala smiled to herself. It had taken years for Gran to make her garden because it was so difficult to find soil or plants, but she had made some soil with rotten vegetables and fruit, and slowly found bits and pieces here and there. Now she spent as much time in the garden as possible, even when it was dark or raining. It was tiny, but full of life; Gran was managing to grow all sorts of plants. At night, little lamps shone, and mirrors reflected their light.

Gran was bending over a tomato plant, but as Sala entered, she straightened up slowly. Sala could see from her face that it hurt her to move like that. Her back was often painful from when she'd been injured during the Oil Wars, so she almost never left the apartment these days.

Sala greeted her, then held out her hand. "Gran, I have something for you!"

Gran frowned. "For me?"

Sala nodded, giving her the small plastic package. "I think it must be something for you to plant."

Gran looked down at the strange gift, and to Sala's surprise, her face went deathly pale. For one awful moment, she thought Gran might even fall over.

"Gran! Are you OK?" Sala put an arm around her, and made her sit down on the little bench that looked over the city.

Gran's face went
deathly pale.

Gran's lips were trembling. "Where... Sala, where did you get this?" she whispered.

"A woman gave it to me. On the walkway. Well, just off the walkway, really. I think she must have followed me. Why? What is it? What does it mean?"

Gran didn't answer. Instead, she turned the package over, looking for a way to open it. She broke it down the middle, and the little dried fruit fell out into her hand.

"It's a fruit of the wild rose," she said in a low voice, touching it carefully. "And the thing is... wild roses don't grow in the city."

Sala frowned. "So, where did it come from?" Gran, still pale, said nothing.

Sala was thinking fast. "You don't mean... it came from *outside*?"

Sala had never seen anything from beyond the city. Everything they ate, everything they used – it was all grown or made within the city's limits. What's more, there was a force field at the city boundary that was impossible to cross: there were alarms there that sensed your wrist chip before you even got close, and then government agents appeared in seconds to arrest you. They did not want anyone going into the contaminated world beyond – it was much too dangerous, they said.

The color was beginning to come back into Gran's face now. "Wild roses used to grow near our house, when I was young," she told Sala. "Before the Oil Wars."

"Your house near the beach?" said Sala. Gran was always talking about how she'd lived by the ocean when she was a child.

"That's right," said Gran. "My brother and I used to play with the fruit. There are tiny hairs inside that make you want to scratch. So we used to play tricks with them: put them in people's clothes. Oh, we had a lot of fun!" Gran laughed gently. "But then… we grew up. And the wars started."

"So, your brother – that's… Great-Uncle Eston, right?" said Sala. "The one you tell stories about? The one who…"

"Died." Gran nodded. "After the Oil Wars, I looked for him all over the city, but I couldn't find him anywhere. I've always believed that he died in the outside world, in the contamination." She rolled the fruit between her fingers. "I haven't heard from him for more than… thirty years. Until – this."

Sala frowned. "Wait a minute – you think your *brother* sent the fruit?"

Gran smiled. "Oh, I know it's silly, isn't it? I don't know where it came from. I would love to believe it's from him. But…" She shook her head sadly. "How could it be?"

The idea was crazy. But it was also exciting. "Gran, you never know! Maybe there *are* places outside the city that didn't get contaminated – where people survived."

Gran looked out at the view of towering blocks, stretching into the distance. Her mind seemed far away. Then she turned to Sala. "Did the woman say how you could contact her?"

"The woman?"

"The one who gave you the fruit."

"Oh! No. She disappeared."

"Right. Well, that's that, then," said Gran. "Maybe someone found it in a dusty corner and thought of my little garden… But it's very odd, all the same."

She got up and returned to her tomato plants, taking off the dead and dying leaves from the bottom of each one. "So, tell me about your day," she said, over her shoulder. "Did you have a nice time with Cham?"

"Oh, Gran!" said Sala. "You know we've been together a year today? Well, he bought us a pod experience. We're going to swim with dolphins."

"Are you?" Gran sounded surprised. "He's such a kind boy. But I don't know how he can afford something like that."

"I know." Sala thought of Cham's face when he left her, and felt uneasy. "I don't understand it either."

Gran threw a handful of leaves onto a pile in the corner. "Well, it's good to be generous," she said. "And swimming with dolphins is wonderful – although this isn't quite the real thing, of course."

"You've been swimming with dolphins?" asked Sala.

"Yes. Years ago, before the Oil Wars," said Gran. "When I went traveling with your grandfather."

Gran was always talking about the days when she and Sala's grandfather used to travel to distant lands, climb mountains, and go swimming in the ocean. Such adventures had been normal then, but they seemed almost magical now.

"Do you think we'll ever be able to travel like you did?" Sala asked. "Me and Cham?"

Gran looked thoughtful. "Who knows?" she said. "Maybe one day. If we're ever free of these silly things." She tapped her wrist.

Sala smiled. Gran had a chip buried under her skin like everyone else, but she wore a bracelet to hide it as a small way of protesting about the government's tight control over everyone.

"You're such a rebel, Gran."

Her gran's eyes danced. "Never give up hope, my love."

3

Pod Life

Back inside the apartment, Sala found her nine-year-old brother Apat playing games on the ultranet in his room. Their mom was still out at work.

Sala went to her own tiny room, and played her ultranet messages. There was one from Niki, but nothing from Cham, so she began a message to him. "Hey," she said. "Did you get home OK?" Then she stopped. *Had* he been odd with her? She wasn't sure. Maybe it was silly to think so. Then she thought about Gran's fruit.

Don't mention that on the ultranet, she told herself. If it really *was* from outside, it could be dangerous to say anything about it. "Please message me," she finished instead. "I'm dying to tell you a story about Gran. Missing you."

She began watching an ultranet story-stream. Story-streams were a little like the movies that people watched in the past. This one was very exciting, but Sala couldn't concentrate. The conversation with Gran had gotten her thinking.

Will we ever be free? she wondered. *Or will we only ever see the world virtually?* Of course, the virtual world was interesting. There was so much you could see on the ultranet or at the simulator center. But afterward, you were still in the city in a tiny room, surrounded by thousands of other people doing exactly the same thing. Was this the best life they could hope for?

A call came in on Sala's ultranet connection, and her heart jumped.

"Cham!"

His face on her virtual interface looked worried. "Hi, Sala. Are you busy?"

"Not really. Just a story-stream. Why?"

"Well... I've been... thinking." The color rose in his face.

"Thinking about what?" demanded Sala. So there *was* something wrong. "Cham, has something happened?"

"No, no, no. It's nothing, really. I just thought you might be annoyed with me, and I didn't want to ruin our day."

Sala laughed. "When am I ever annoyed with you?"

"You might be this time." Cham hesitated. "It's just... that pod thing."

Suddenly, Sala thought she understood. "Cham, I know. You shouldn't have bought us such an expensive present – I mean, it's wonderful, but you don't have enough money. We can get what you paid for this back, I'm sure..."

"But that's the problem," said Cham. "I didn't pay for it all."

"Sorry?"

"It was a special offer – if you bought one experience, you could get another for free." He suddenly started talking very fast. "I had enough money for one, and you just had to say you were interested in Pod Life. So I thought, hey, yes – that's a great idea, I don't have to actually *do* it—"

"Stop, stop!" cried Sala. "Slow down a minute."

There was a second of silence.

"Cham," said Sala. "Is this the Pod Life that Ding was talking about? The one where you live in a pod for two years?"

Cham looked uncomfortable. "Yes."

"And you said you were interested, to get this special offer?"

"Yes."

"So... *are* you interested?"

"No! Well, I mean – just as an idea, you know..."

"You didn't say you'd do it, did you?" she whispered.

"No! No, of course not." He paused. "You said you hated the idea. When we were with the others."

"Oh." So *that's* why he was quiet. Nothing more serious. Sala felt a rush of gladness. "Why would I mind you getting a special offer? It's cool."

Cham's face brightened. "Phew! So we're OK? And I'll see you at the energy center tomorrow, with Apat?"

"Of course," said Sala. "See you then."

As soon as Cham's face disappeared, she suddenly remembered: Gran's story! She'd forgotten to tell him about it in the end.

■ ■ ■ ■

Sala and Apat arrived at the energy center before it opened, and found Cham already in line to get in. The center was always busy, because everyone was eager to earn energy units. You could run, ride a bicycle, climb, or jump on different machines, which created energy, so then you added the units to your wrist chip. You never earned many, but it was better than nothing – and a good way to exercise, and get out of your apartment.

Sala knew that Apat loved it when Cham came with them to the center, because Cham always joked around with him. The three of them laughed and talked as they waited for the doors to open. Then they were in, and heading to their favorite machines. Apat chose the jumping machines, as always; Cham got onto a climbing machine and was soon halfway up a wall. Sala stepped onto a running machine, and started to run.

After thirty minutes, Apat was still jumping up and down happily, but Sala and Cham took a break and went to the café, where a drinks machine made special mixtures of juice and energy liquids.

"I'll buy these," said Sala. "It's my turn."

When she came back to their table, Cham was watching something on the ultranet.

"Hey," said Sala. "Drinks here!"

"Sorry," said Cham, looking back at Sala hurriedly. "And thanks. Climbing is thirsty work." But there was something odd in his voice again, and a strange expression on his face.

"What were you watching?" asked Sala.

"Oh, nothing. It's just annoying. Stupid messages."

"Who from?" Sala was surprised.

"From the Pod Life people. Because I said I was interested."

"Can't you just get rid of them?"

"Well, yes." He bit his lip. "But I've read a lot of them and… they kind of make me think. Maybe this Pod Life thing wouldn't be so bad, after all. You can earn a lot of money for it – a real salary, like your mom's."

Sala stared at him. "You're not serious?"

He reached out for her hand. "Hey, don't look at me like that. It's just an idea. I mentioned it to Mom last night and… well, she surprised me. She was really enthusiastic."

Sala's mouth dropped open. "So you *were* thinking about it!" she cried. "You were thinking about it the whole time!"

"I wasn't! You don't understand—"

"Last night, you said it was just to get the second pod experience!"

"It *was*—"

"It doesn't sound like that." Sala banged her drink down. "You've read the messages, you've thought about it, you've even talked to your *mom*—"

Cham spread his hands. "Sala, please. I'm only talking. Honestly, I don't know what your problem is."

Cham reached out for Sala's hand.

"What?" Sala stared at him. "You're thinking of leaving me for two whole years and you can't see the problem?"

■ ■ ■ ■

They had never argued before. Ever. When Sala got home with Apat, she felt sick. She managed not to say anything in front of her little brother, but Gran could see at once that she was upset.

"Something is wrong, isn't it?" asked Gran, as they sat in the Real Space. "You look very pale."

Sala explained everything – about the special offer, and their conversation at the energy center.

"I was so upset. We argued, and I told Apat we had to leave early," she finished miserably. "Gran, I can't believe he's even considering it." Her eyes filled with tears. "*Two years!*"

"It's normal to consider things, Sala. It doesn't mean he'll actually do it. I'm sure he loves you, but you can't blame him for thinking about the future. You have to remember that his situation is different from yours. Think about where he lives. It costs a lot to live in an earth apartment – you need constant lighting and heating. And when there's so little work available, most people have no hope of changing their lives. They're trapped. Your mother is in a very unusual position, you know – Cham's dad only gets bits and pieces of work now and then. So Cham probably needs to think about the future more carefully than you."

Sala thought for a while. It was true, her family was very lucky, and she sometimes forgot that. Her mom was a food scientist in the meat-growing laboratory, developing different kinds of meat from just a few animal cells. It meant that she earned a regular salary, unlike Cham's parents, who were always worrying about money. That was how Sala and her family were able to live in their rooftop apartment.

"You're right. I need to say sorry. Thanks, Gran."

"Any time." Then Gran hesitated. "Um… you didn't see anyone else today, did you?"

"No… it was just me and Apat, and Cham."

"I mean… well, I suppose I'm silly to ask. I mean the woman you saw yesterday. The one who gave you the fruit."

"Oh! No." Sala's thoughts had been so full of Cham and Pod Life that she'd almost forgotten about it. "Do you honestly think it came from outside?"

Gran stared into the distance for a moment, deep in thought. "Well… there's nowhere in the city for wild roses to grow. But of course it can't have come in from outside… unless…" She waved her hand. "Oh, don't listen to me."

"But I love listening to you!"

Gran smiled. "Well, I suppose I'm thinking that maybe, just maybe, there *is* still life in the outside world – and maybe someone from that world has found a way across the city boundary."

It was an extraordinary idea. Sala thought of all the places she'd visited in the simulator. Some of them were really beautiful, but you couldn't really explore them because you were still in a little room with a time limit. How wonderful to think that there might still be a different world out there – a world where you could do all those things for real!

4

Cham's Idea

Sala went back down to her room and sent Cham a message. "Hi, Cham. I'm really sorry I got so angry," she said. "It was stupid. Can we talk? I'll come over, if you like."

Then she waited for his reply. Five minutes went by. Then ten. Fifteen. Sala bit her lip anxiously. What if he wouldn't forgive her? She had really shouted at him, and now she felt awful. Of course, Gran was right. She couldn't judge him for considering Pod Life. She was in the wrong, and now she'd probably ruined everything.

She sat on the edge of her bed, worrying. She tried to think of something else instead. The mystery woman: *Who was she? How did she know about Gran?* She wondered when she would see her again...

A message – from Cham! His smiling face, saying simply: "Can you come to mine?" Sala's heart flooded with happiness. Forgetting about the woman, she jumped to her feet and rushed out. It wasn't far to Cham's apartment block, but another storm had gathered. The skies were heavy and gray as stone; Sala heard a clap of thunder. Too bad, she thought.

She arrived just as the rain began to pour, and lightning flashed across the sky. She dived through the doors and jumped into the elevator. Down, down... nine floors down, she stepped out into a different world. It was so quiet and calm: a world the storm couldn't reach. At Cham's door, she stood by the recognition screen and waited.

The door opened. Cham stood there, his arms open, and Sala rushed into a huge hug. Hand in hand, they went inside the apartment. It was a bit smaller than Sala's, with no windows – and no garden either, of course. Cham's parents had furnished it nicely, and there were plenty of lights to make it bright. But it was crowded because Cham had two younger sisters, and Sala knew they all hated living deep underground – especially Cham's dad Tian.

"Do you want me to put the hologram on?" asked Cham. "No one else is around."

One wall of the apartment was just plain white, with a hologram you could turn on and off. There was a choice of lifelike views in 3D – not as clever as the illusions in the simulator, but they did help the family to forget, at times, that they lived deep under the ground.

"Don't use any energy units for me – I'm not bothered," said Sala.

Then she and Cham both began talking at once.

"Look, I know I was wrong—"

"Sorry, I don't want to—"

They both stopped, and laughed.

"I don't want to argue again," said Sala. "It was horrible. And I want to know more about this Pod Life thing."

"OK… if you're sure."

"Go for it."

"Right. Well, they say it's a huge study opportunity. You learn things in a completely different way because your whole body is involved. You don't just learn the ideas. You actually *experience* them."

Sala frowned, trying to imagine it.

"Then the other thing is, you get loads of energy units," Cham carried on. "Because you're just lying in the pod, they're able to store all the heat energy that your body creates. Then you get it all back as energy units when you come out. And they pay you, too. Or your family instead, if you want."

His voice was full of enthusiasm, and Sala began to feel uneasy. It all made too much sense. Then she thought of Gran.

"But Cham," she said, "what if there was a better future – something completely different?"

"What do you mean?"

"Well, it's just… you know that fruit the woman gave me?"

"What about it?"

"Gran said she thought it had come from… outside."

"Outside what?" Cham looked confused.

"The city, of course!"

Cham's mouth dropped open. Then he threw back his head and laughed. "That is the craziest thing I've ever heard!"

"Well, Gran doesn't seem to think so…"

"Come on, are you joking? Your gran is fantastic. I love the way she talks about the past and all that. But that fruit – someone must have found it in a closet or somewhere."

"Well… maybe," said Sala. "But who would have sent it without a note? Gran thinks… she thinks maybe it came from her long-lost brother. My Great-Uncle Eston."

"From her brother?" Cham paused for a second, then laughed. "But I mean… come on… an old dried fruit?"

Sala studied his face. He wasn't taking Gran's suggestion seriously. He truly didn't believe the fruit came from another world beyond the city boundary – and she couldn't really blame him. This was the only world they were ever likely to experience. Apart from the virtual world, of course… She decided that they needed to talk about something different, because she'd come here to make things better, not worse.

"I wish someone else in your family could do the pod thing," she said. "Your dad, maybe. I can see that all those units and the extra money would be useful. You could move out of here. Your parents could rent a sky apartment instead."

Cham nodded. "My dad couldn't do it, though. It's for people our age: seventeen to twenty-one."

There was a silence. Sala realized now that Cham was ambitious. He wanted to get on in life. She would never want to prevent that – there were so few opportunities to succeed. But she hated the thought of losing him.

"Sala," said Cham, "you know I'd love to help my parents. When I told Mom about it, she looked so hopeful I thought she'd cry. It was awful. But I don't want to leave you."

His words made Sala feel ashamed. Cham had so many things to consider, far more than her.

"I just wondered…" Cham hesitated. "I know what you said before, but… would you think about doing it with me?"

He asked her gently, but his words still came as a shock. Until now, Sala hadn't even thought about doing it herself. She wanted to tell Cham right away that she hated the idea. But then she thought of her Gran, and what she'd said about Cham's situation. Sala needed to consider this, at least.

"So… how would it work?" she asked. "If we were both in a pod, how would we be together?"

"I'm not really sure," Cham confessed. "But I think it's like another world. A virtual world where we can see each other and talk and everything. So at least if we were both doing the same thing, it would almost feel like we were together."

It was a few moments before Sala spoke. Then she looked at Cham and smiled. "Well, we're going to have a pod experience together, right? Then we'll know how it feels. We can think about it more clearly afterward."

5

Swimming with Dolphins

"So, when are you going to the pod center?" asked Niki. "You lucky thing! I'd *love* a pod experience."

It was Monday, and the two friends were riding the walkway home from college. They only attended one day a week; on the other days, they studied virtually, on the ultranet. Studying at home helped with overcrowding, used less energy, and made teaching easier: well, that's what the government said.

"Tomorrow afternoon," Sala told her.

"I'm jealous!" Niki said. "In fact, I've been looking into that Pod Life thing that Ding told us about. It sounds great. I'm not old enough yet, though. You have to be seventeen and I've still got two months to go."

Sala looked at her friend. Another one! The news had spread about Pod Life, and other students had been discussing it all weekend. Many seemed to see it as a serious choice.

"Really?" she replied. "Has everyone gone crazy?"

Niki laughed. "Not at all. Think of all those energy units! Why don't you like the idea?"

Sala frowned. She was still looking forward to the dolphin experience. That was exciting. But whenever she thought about lying in a pod for months, her stomach seemed to turn over and over – in spite of what she'd told Cham.

"I suppose it seems to me like losing control," she said.

"Well, I guess you're not the only one who's afraid."

Sala was a bit offended. "I'm not talking about being *afraid*. I like to be independent, that's all. The government controls us enough already. I'd rather be free than in a pod."

"But isn't that the point?" suggested Niki. "Once you've got all those energy units and extra money, you *are* free. More free than you were before."

"Not really," said Sala. "And two years of your life is a high price to pay."

"Pod Life is the future, Sala." Niki sounded very confident. "In a few years, everyone will be doing it. I don't want to be left behind – do you?"

"Well, no, I guess not." Sala looked away. They had almost reached Sala's exit, so she gathered her things together and said goodbye to Niki. But as she stepped off the walkway, she felt a hand touching her back.

"Did your grandmother like it?" whispered a voice.

Sala looked around, and gasped. It was the woman who had given her the fruit.

"Yeah… uh, yes," she managed to say. "She did. But who are you? Where did it come from?"

"You'll find out soon. I'll see you again."

And then, just like the first time, the woman stepped quickly onto the walkway and was soon lost among the crowds.

It was maddening. What was going on? Was it some kind of game? Sala wondered whether to tell Gran, but there was nothing new to say. Gran was so excited; it would be awful if this was all a cruel joke. *I'll see you again*, the woman had said: well, then, there was really nothing to do but wait.

■ ■ ■ ■

The following afternoon, as Sala walked up and down in her little room, waiting to go with Cham for their pod experience, she had a strange feeling in her stomach. Maybe this was how it felt to go on a *real* journey, she thought. You were excited and you couldn't concentrate on anything else, but you were also a tiny bit afraid. In a good way.

From far down on the ground floor, Cham sent a message: "Ready when you are!"

Sala rushed down, and they set out on one of the fastest walkways to the pod center, talking happily. Now that they were actually on their way, it was all so much fun.

"We're like explorers from the past," she said.

"Yeah. Heading out on an expedition!" Cham laughed.

"Maybe there'll be more than dolphins." Sala let her mind go wild. "There'll be tigers and other dangerous animals and... and... snow!"

"Take it easy, crazy girl!" said Cham. "In the ocean?"

"Hmmm."

"But who knows what there might be under the water!" laughed Cham."

"Oh! Don't say that," cried Sala. "I'll worry about it and then I won't be able to swim."

"*Can* you swim?" asked Cham, curiously.

"Um, no. Can you?"

Cham shook his head. "No. But that's the fantastic thing. Everything is possible in a pod."

They left the walkway at the nearest exit to the pod center. The building was enormous, higher even than the tallest apartment blocks. Sala had seen it before, of course, from a distance – but she'd never been so close to it.

"Wow!" she said.

"I know," said Cham. "Come on. This is it."

The door recognized that they had tickets, and let them in. Inside, the lights were so bright they were almost blinding, and there was a constant soft noise of people working on computers. All the technicians wore white coats; they looked serious and professional. One wall was invisible – all you could see was a huge 3D hologram advertising Pod Life.

They didn't have long to wait. A friendly young woman called Zee guided them to their pod area.

"These are your body suits," Zee told them. "You can change over there." She handed them each a slippery, silvery suit and pointed them in the right direction.

Sala and Cham each went into a little room, and Sala put on her suit, made a neat pile of her clothes, and carried them out to Zee. Cham was already there, looking more gorgeous than ever in his silver suit.

"Good," smiled Zee. "Let's go, shall we?"

She led them toward a row of strange-looking pods that stood vertically. Sala frowned. Would it really feel like she was swimming with dolphins in one of those?

"You just walk in," Zee explained. "And then, when everything is attached, the pod moves into a horizontal position, so you're lying down."

"Here goes," said Cham, his eyes shining with excitement. "See you in an hour, Sala!"

"Sooner than that. You'll see her in the pod," remarked Zee.

Zee guided Sala into her pod; the door closed, and she could feel the cool metal attachments touching her face and her body suit. *Whoosh*. All at once, she was floating in warm, clear water. A gentle wave splashed her face. She licked her lips and tasted salt. She was in the ocean!

Above her, the sky was a perfect, cloudless blue. In one direction, a golden beach was just visible, with the tops of green trees beyond it. In another direction, the ocean stretched out into the distance. Cautiously, she tried moving her arms and legs, and found that it came naturally. She could swim!

It was such a lovely sensation. She grew braver, and began to swim more rapidly toward the beach.

Then she heard a noise. *Click-click-click-click-click. Wheeee!*

The sound was traveling through the water. And there it was again. *Wheeee!* A loud, clear whistle, right by her ear. Sala turned her head, and gasped. She couldn't believe it – she was face to face with a beautiful gray dolphin. It opened its mouth, and Sala felt sure it was greeting her.

The dolphin whistled again, then turned away, its back making an arch in the water. It disappeared under the surface for a moment, so Sala looked around.

And there was Cham. He was swimming toward her with a dolphin on either side of him.

"Sala!" he called.

She waved excitedly. "I think they want us to follow them!"

Sure enough, the dolphins set off, their smooth, strong bodies sliding through the ocean. Sala and Cham swam with them for a while – further out into the ocean first, and then back toward the beach. When the water became shallower, the dolphins began to swim lazily in circles.

Floating gently, Sala looked down into the water's depths. "Oh, wow!" she cried. "Cham! Look!"

There, below the surface, were hundreds of multicolored fish. Blue, red, yellow, orange, purple, silver, and gold.

"Gorgeous!" breathed Cham.

They watched as the fish moved slowly between the waving ocean plants, silent and peaceful in their watery world.

While Sala and Cham were watching the fish, the dolphins carried on making a huge variety of sounds – whistles and clicks and strange, wild calls. It was magical.

"They're talking to us," laughed Sala.

"I think they want us to follow them!"

"Or singing!" Cham suggested.

Sala rolled onto her back and lay floating, staring up at the sky. It was so perfect here. She wondered about the land in the distance. Maybe it was an island. An island with fruit trees and birds singing. A place of calm and beauty and peace.

She began to swim again, next to Cham. He held on to a dolphin's tail and it began to play with him, pulling him along much faster than he could swim. Sala did the same with another dolphin and they had a lot of fun, diving down through the water and back up to the surface with a splash.

Then the biggest dolphin moved toward Sala and pushed her with its nose. She looked deep into its eyes, and reached out to touch its face. Its expression was so wise. Time seemed to stop. *I'm connected to an ancient time and place*, thought Sala. This was such an intelligent, sensitive creature, who seemed to know exactly who she was.

And then she heard a voice: "Your hour is almost over. Your pod is about to move back into a vertical position."

The ocean disappeared. Cham disappeared. There was nothing at all. Then the pod moved, and Sala was standing again. She tried to move her arms, but they were trapped. She wanted to fight, or run, but she couldn't lift her legs.

"Help! I'm—" she began.

"Sala! Sala, it's OK," said someone.

White, gray, silver... Shining glass. Then a face she had seen before. Zee's face.

"Hey, Sala," said Zee, her voice soft and calm. "You're back. No need to worry. Did you have a wonderful trip?"

Sala tried to breathe more calmly. It was OK. Nothing wrong. She was back. The attachments came off and she walked out of the pod, her knees trembling. She touched the silvery suit. It was completely dry.

No water. No ocean. Just sensations. A wave of shock hit her. It was all too much. She buried her face in her hands, and burst into tears.

6

Sala's Decision

Fifteen minutes later, Sala was dressed in her own clothes again, and was sitting next to Cham near the changing rooms. She was still feeling a bit shaky.

Zee brought them a high-energy drink. "Here you are. Drink this. And take your time," she told them. "It's normal to feel a little strange when you first come out."

"I don't feel strange," said Cham. "Fantastic, more like! That was the best thing I've ever done in my life. Unreal."

"It was unreal, all right," remarked Sala weakly.

Cham laughed, and then looked at her anxiously. "But you did enjoy it, right?"

"Oh yes. It was... extraordinary." Sala paused. "Much better than I expected, to be honest. When the dolphins started playing with us, it was out of this world."

Cham's eyes danced. "Yeah, really great. And I loved it right at the end, when that big dolphin came up to you and lifted you out of the water."

Sala frowned. The big dolphin had only touched her gently, and looked into her eyes. "He didn't lift me."

"But I saw him do it. That's odd."

Sala felt puzzled. "Yes. I mean... it was *you* in there, wasn't it? Your voice sounded a bit different, but apart from that..."

"Sure it was me," said Cham. "I guess they take a 3D picture of you inside the pod, and then they create an avatar."

"But an avatar isn't *us*. It's an imitation of us."

Cham nodded. "Yes, but it's controlled by our thoughts. And we were in the same virtual space together. You remember following the dolphins to see the fish, right?"

"Yes."

"And then the dolphins were making all that noise, and we laughed about them talking to us—"

"Singing!" Sala nodded.

"That's right!"

"So it *was* you. And me. Us." Sala felt a bit better.

"We were communicating through our avatars," said Cham "It's so clever."

A bit too clever, said a voice in Sala's head: they'd been together, and yet not together; they were able to talk to each other, but sometimes experienced things separately. It was confusing, and a bit frightening.

She stood up and stretched. Her legs had stopped trembling, more or less, and she wanted to get out of there. "Can we go?"

"OK. I'll just finish this." Cham swallowed his drink hurriedly, and they waved goodbye to Zee.

As they passed the enormous hologram wall by the entrance, Cham put his arm around Sala. She wished they could just go back to normal now. But on the walkway home, he didn't talk as much as usual. He looked out over the city and seemed to be thinking deeply. It worried Sala. There was a big conversation coming, and she wasn't looking forward to it.

They were almost home when Cham turned to her.

"You know what," he said. "If I didn't have you, I'd sign up for Pod Life, I think."

"You would?"

"Yeah. I thought it was cool. But... we want to be together, right?"

"Right."

"And you're the one with doubts about it, so you should

decide. I would do it – but only if you want to do it, too. If you don't, that's it. We won't."

Sala stared at him. "But… what if I say no?"

"That's OK."

"You just said you'd like to do it."

"Not without you," repeated Cham. "Look, I trust you, Sala. You'll make a good decision, I know you will."

Sala looked at Cham's face. She loved him so much. They'd never had to make a big decision like this before, and she wished with all her heart that he wasn't making her choose. But she could see he was only being fair.

"All right, Cham," she said slowly. "I'll think about it. I promise."

When Sala arrived home, Mom was back from work, and Apat and Gran were there, too. They all sat down to eat and talk together. It was a delicious dinner – Mom had brought home some top-quality meat from the laboratory, and Gran had added some vegetables from her garden. Everyone wanted to hear about Sala's pod experience, so she described it slowly, giving every last detail. Apat's eyes grew wide as saucers. "Ohhhh. *I* want to go!"

Sala smiled. "You would love it, Apat. But you'll have to save some money first."

"That's right," Mom agreed. "Oh, it's good to see you all and really talk. I've been so busy at work the last few days, I feel I've not been home much at all."

"Is that because of the packing equipment breaking?" asked Sala. "Niki and I passed the laboratory the other day – there were loads of people looking for work."

"Yes, the breakdown has caused so many problems," said Mom. "I feel very sorry for all those people. But we have all the technicians we need. And they keep bringing in more robots."

"That's what I told Niki." Sala hesitated. "Mom, I've been wondering what you think of this new thing, Pod Life. You've heard about it, haven't you?"

Mom nodded. "Yes, of course."

"Is it a good idea?" asked Sala.

"Well, they say they're offering high-level studies, so that's obviously good," said Mom cautiously. "But living in a pod... it's hard to say. Real life is difficult, but it's... what we have."

Gran nodded wisely.

Sala took a deep breath. "So... what would you say if Cham and I wanted to do it?"

Gran and Mom looked at each other. There was silence. At last, Mom spoke. "I'd ask you to think about the things you love. And the people you'd leave behind. We'd miss you terribly, and I think you'd miss us." Mom smiled. "I wouldn't stop you, Sala. But I'd be sad. And I'd wish with all my heart that there was something better for you."

Sala nodded. "Thanks, Mom."

Then Gran spoke up. "And remember, Sala, maybe there *will* be something better, one day. There's more to the world than this city, believe me. If that rose fruit came from outside, who knows what may be possible."

Sala's mom looked uncertain. "I don't think you can depend on that, Gran," she said. "We shouldn't raise our hopes."

"No, no, you're quite right. I'm just saying – maybe the world out there is not as terrible as the government would like us to believe."

Gran said nothing more, but her eyes were shining. Sala realized that for Gran, the rose fruit meant something real; it spoke of a world that Sala could only begin to imagine. And what if – just what if – she was right?

For the next twenty-four hours, Sala tried to think clearly. She had to consider Cham's future, not just her own. The questions went around and around in her head. At last, she knew she couldn't put off her decision any longer, and when she'd finished her studies on the day after the pod experience, she invited Cham to her apartment.

It was pouring with rain again, and his hair and clothes were wet when he arrived.

"Look at you!" said Sala.

"I know," said Cham, "but I think it's just stopping. Hopefully we can still go up to the Real Space?"

"Sure."

Up on the roof, they talked about all the things that didn't really matter: what they'd eaten for dinner, the weather, Apat on the jumping machine… all to avoid the one big thing they needed to discuss.

Then Sala forced herself to be brave. "I heard that Palo has done the same as you. Got a pod ticket, I mean."

Cham nodded. "Yeah… so has Ding."

"So they'll end up doing Pod Life."

"Probably. Yeah."

They fell silent. Sala swallowed. This was harder than she'd imagined. "Cham, I've made a decision," she said, in a rush.

"I thought so." He played with her fingers, matching them against his. "Go on."

"You really will be OK with what I say?"

"Try me."

Sala bit her lip. "OK. So… Cham, I can't do it. I'm really sorry. I know it's a big opportunity, but… I just can't. For lots of reasons. I loved the pod, but I'd be afraid of doing it for longer. It was too… strange. And I can't leave Gran and Mom and Apat." She hesitated. Should she mention the wild rose fruit again? She wasn't sure. But then she opened her mouth and the words just came out. "Also, I know you think it's crazy, but… the fruit thing… well, it's given me hope."

As soon as she said it, she wished she hadn't.

"It's a *little* bit crazy," said Cham. But he didn't laugh.

Sala nodded. "I know. Sorry. It's not really about that… it's all the other things…"

"Look," said Cham. "It doesn't matter what your reasons are. I know you've thought about it, and I can see you've decided the answer is no. That's enough. I meant what I said."

It was good to hear him say it again so clearly.

"Thank you," she said. "But you have to be sure, Cham. It's going to be hard. If Palo and Ding sign up… and Niki, too, as soon as she's seventeen… we'll be on our own."

"We have each other," said Cham. "What else do we need?"

Sala smiled. "A future, maybe?"

"Well, yes." He laughed.

Sala looked out at the view: nothing but black and silver tower blocks against the cold gray sky. "If there's a better world out there, we have to find it."

"I love that you're so hopeful." Cham drew her close, and kissed her. "And I'm so proud of you. It wasn't really fair to give you such a tough decision to make, but I knew you'd be strong enough."

Sala closed her eyes and kissed him back. It was the first important crossroads they'd come to together. It felt like a moment of magic: they'd never been so close.

7

A Difficult Choice

"**A**re you two crazy?" Niki couldn't believe it. "*Neither* of you?"

"Nope," said Sala.

"But I thought you loved your pod experience."

"So what? It was an hour, not two years."

Niki shook her head. "I'll never understand you."

"Oooh, I hope not," laughed Sala.

It was Monday, and Sala and Niki were at college again. A few days had passed since Sala's decision, and she was feeling happy about it. Happy and at peace. Many of the other students still talked about nothing but Pod Life, but she didn't care.

Now, she was sitting with Niki on their lunch break, and thinking about the months ahead.

"I'm counting the weeks until I can sign up," Niki told her. "But maybe I'd feel differently if I were in love."

Sala felt herself go pink. "It's not just that," she protested. All the reasons she'd given to Cham ran through her mind, but how could she explain them to Niki? It was really complicated.

Back at home that afternoon, Sala thought about Niki's words: it was true that because she was with Cham, life felt exciting. She smiled to herself. She'd been about to do some studying, but watching a love story-stream was a much better idea. She chose one that Cham had recommended, about the Oil Wars. Feeling warm and comfortable and sleepy, she thought of Cham, holding her in the Real Space. His arms always felt so wonderful… With the story-stream still playing, her eyes slowly began to shut.

She was asleep when her ultranet began to beep. *Maybe it's part of the story*, she thought sleepily – but then a light started flashing, and she opened her eyes.

Urgent message.

Sala sat up hurriedly, and opened the message. It was from Cham.

"Can you meet me now at the simulator center? I want to talk face to face. Love you."

Sala splashed some cold water on her face to wake herself up, and then hurried to the simulator center. Cham sent her another message while she was on her way to say that he was in Space 46, and when she went in, he'd already chosen an illusion. He was standing on a rocky seashore, with gray waves crashing in. White seabirds flew close to the surface of the water, fighting against the wind. Sala gasped. It was cold.

She touched his arm. "Cham."

Cham pulled Sala toward him. "Thank you for coming," he whispered. "I'm sorry."

"Sorry for what?"

"It's my dad." Cham's voice broke.

"Your dad? What's wrong? Is he sick?"

"No." Cham looked out over the rough ocean. "It's his work."

"But I thought you said he was helping fix this problem at the meat laboratory," said Sala.

"He was," said Cham.

"So…?"

"So they decided not to fix the old equipment. They've brought in a new design instead. They'll never need him again."

Sala was puzzled. "Why?"

"They've put in new nanobots that stay inside the equipment and check everything, every day. They find problems even before they've happened, and fix them."

Sala began to realize why this news was so awful. Cham's dad Tian knew how to fix the old equipment: that was his job. He hadn't done anything else for years. If this was happening at the meat laboratory, it would soon be happening everywhere, and he wouldn't get any work at all.

"My mom is really upset," Cham carried on. "We're low on energy units already, so it's hard. Dad came home with the news yesterday afternoon, and he and Mom have been really depressed ever since."

"I'm so sorry," she said. She felt awful. *Sorry* just wasn't enough.

Cham nodded. "I know. And the thing is…"

He stopped, and Sala realized what he was going to say.

"Pod Life," she said.

Cham looked desperately miserable. "You guessed."

"Cham, no!"

"Sala… I don't have a choice."

"There's always a choice."

"Tell me, then!" he demanded, suddenly sounding bitter. "Tell me what else I should do."

"We'll find something."

"Like what? Like *what*, exactly?"

Sala's mind was racing. If only she'd seen that woman again…

"We don't know yet. But I'd really miss you – and so would your family…" She bit her lip.

"I'll be doing it *for* my family," Cham pointed out. "You can see that, can't you?"

"I'll be doing it for my family," Cham pointed out.

Sala nodded. "Yes. Yes. Sorry." All at once, she was trembling. Trembling from the cold, and from the shock, and from unhappiness. She sat down and hugged her knees.

"Sorry, Sala," said Cham. "Let me change this horrible illusion." He went to the screen on the wall, and changed the scenery to a sunny park. Then he came and sat next to her. "Sorry for getting angry. I'm not angry with you. Especially not with you. I'm just angry with life."

"It's OK. I know." She looked at him. "So, is that it? You've decided? For sure?"

Cham was silent for a moment. "Like I said, I don't know what else to do." Then he turned to her. "The only thing I can ask is this: if I do Pod Life without you, will you still be here for me when I come out? Can you wait two years?"

His words felt like an earthquake breaking open their lives. Sala started to cry. It was too cruel. She rested her head on her knees and let the tears flow.

At last, she looked up. "Cham, you have to do what's right for you. I'm not going to stop you. And of course I'll wait."

When she and Cham left the simulator center, it was still only late afternoon, so Sala went to the energy center. All she wanted to do was run. Run and run and run. She ran until she was exhausted – too tired to think anymore.

She wished she could be with Cham, but his family was in crisis; they all needed him more than she did right now. As she walked home, loneliness hit her. This was how it would be, for two whole years… Self-pity rose like a wave inside her.

"Hey! Careful!" cried a man.

Sala hadn't been looking where she was going. She'd bumped straight into the man, who'd dropped a bagful of dried food packets, spreading them everywhere.

"Oh! I'm so sorry!" gasped Sala, and she bent down at once to help him pick them up.

Other people joined in, and the packets were soon gathered together again. As Sala reached for the last one, another hand reached for it at the same time. A thin hand. It touched hers, and Sala saw that it was already holding something: a little paper note.

It was the woman.

"It's you—" began Sala.

"Shhh!" In one quick, smooth movement, the woman pushed the note between Sala's fingers, nodded at her, and then set off rapidly toward the walkway. But Sala wasn't going to let her disappear this time. She rushed after the woman and caught her arm, holding it tightly.

"Who are you?"

"Let me go." The woman's voice was fierce.

"Tell me who you are first."

"Do you want to put us both in danger?"

Danger? Sala's mouth dropped open. "Of course not. I just want to talk to you."

"Then don't say anything else. Turn around and walk away. Give that to your grandmother." For a second, the woman moved a little closer. "Stay quiet. I'll find you. Soon."

Sala did as the woman had said: she turned and walked down the street. Then she raced up to her apartment and arrived breathless. She found Gran sitting with Mom, talking and drinking tea; for once, Mom had got home from work early.

"Sala! You look like you've seen a ghost!" said Mom. "What's happened?"

Sala didn't know where to start. She handed the note to Gran. "It's from the same woman," she said. Then she sat down and covered her face with her hands. "And Cham is going to do Pod Life without me."

"Oh, Sala!" cried Mom. Then realization crossed her face. "Does this have anything to do with his dad's work?"

"Yes!" said Sala. "Mom, why can't they just use people instead of replacing them with robots and nanobots all the time?" Suddenly, Sala felt more angry than upset. It wasn't fair.

But before Mom could answer, there was a gasp from Gran. She'd opened the note and held it with trembling fingers.

"He's alive!" she whispered. "My brother Eston is alive."

"What?" said Mom, putting down her cup of tea. Sala stared at Gran, who held out the note. Together, Sala and Mom read it.

My dear Malia,

I don't know if you will ever receive this. I've been trying to send a message for many years, but nothing has crossed the boundary successfully. We know you can't leave your city, but now I hear that maybe messages can reach you, if you are still alive. I hope so.

I want you to know that I have a good, happy life with my wife. Our two sons are doing well, and we have three grandchildren. We have a very nice house near the ocean and there are wild roses in the garden, just as there were when we were young. If you received one of the fruits, you know that this is true, and that it came from me. I still smile when I think of all the fun we had as children, playing on the beach and in the forest. But it also makes me so sad. I miss you, Malia. Here, we are free, and we have beauty all around us, but my heart breaks when I think of you trapped in that city, like a bird in a cage.

Thank those who took the risk to find you. We think we can trust them, but we know that this letter could put you in danger. If you are reading it, be glad: it means there is hope. But please, be careful.

Your loving brother,

Eston

8

Passenger Cham

"I have to tell Cham. Before it's too late."

When they had all cried and hugged each other, it was the first thing that Sala thought of.

"Wait." Mom put a hand on Sala's arm.

"Wait for what? He's about to sign up for Pod Life."

"We need to think about this." Mom pointed to the letter. "*Please, be careful*. Uncle Eston is right – this could all be very dangerous."

"But we can trust Cham!" protested Sala. "Anyway, he already knows about the wild rose fruit."

There was a silence.

"I think we need to be cautious," said Gran. "You can tell him, Sala. But ask him to keep quiet about it."

"What about his family?"

"No." Mom shook her head. "We can't spread this news any further. I'm sure Cham's parents are good people, but we don't know them well enough."

Sala let out a long, slow breath. This was going to be hard. How could she ask Cham to keep a secret from his parents?

"We also don't know anything about the people who have brought this message," Gran pointed out. "Who are they? How did they get it across the boundary?"

"The woman said she would find me again soon," said Sala. "She *has* to tell me more then."

"Well, that's good," said Gran. "But meanwhile, we do have to be very careful. Don't mention it on the ultranet, Sala. If the government finds out that messages are getting through the force field and passing across the city boundary, there could be big trouble."

Sala went up to her room and sent a message to Cham: "Need to talk to you. Can we meet tomorrow?"

Cham's face appeared on her virtual interface almost at once.

"I'm going to the pod center with Mom and Dad at 4 p.m. tomorrow to look around. I was going to ask you to come. But we can meet before? Outside, fifteen minutes early?"

"Great," Sala replied immediately.

Sala couldn't wait. That night, and the following day, went very slowly. She counted the minutes until it was time to leave for the pod center. The journey across the city seemed to take forever; but when she arrived, Cham was waiting, hands in pockets. She rushed up to him and gave him an enormous hug.

"Hey, you're cheerful," Cham remarked. "What's up?"

"You'll never guess." Sala looked around. They were so close to the pod center that she was worried there might be government agents nearby. She pulled Cham away from the entrance and quickly told him the news about Gran's letter.

Cham's eyes grew wide. "Great news. Wow! Imagine that: thinking your brother might be alive after all that time."

"Crazy, isn't it?" Sala smiled. "But you have to promise not to tell anyone. Not even your mom and dad."

"No problem," said Cham. "I promise." He took Sala's hand and they walked on a little. "So, what happens next?"

"We don't know yet," said Sala. "We have to wait for the woman to contact us again."

"Ah, right," nodded Cham. "That makes sense."

Sala felt a little bit puzzled. Cham was enthusiastic, but he didn't seem to think the news had anything to do with him.

"So… you're still going to do this?" she demanded, waving

her hand toward the pod center.

"Why not? I told you – I have to."

"But don't you see? This changes everything. There's another world out there. The government has lied to us – it's not contaminated like we've been told. We just have to find a way to get there…"

Cham laughed, a little sadly. "Yes, Sala. We're all going to fly over the force field and live happily ever after in a forest where the trees grow gold-covered fruit."

Sala bit her lip. "Ouch," she said.

"Sorry. It's just that… I have to live in the real world, Sala."

"Living in a pod isn't real," said Sala fiercely. "It's the least real thing you could possibly do. It's *virtual* reality. That's the point."

"Hey, hey," said Cham softly. "I don't want to argue. And I don't want to hurt you."

Sala suddenly felt like crying. Here they were, almost at the doors of the pod center. What more could she say? Cham's number one consideration right now was his family, and she couldn't stand in the way of that; but she wished that he would at least *think* about other possibilities.

Cham's parents Dani and Tian were waiting for them just inside. A Pod Life technician greeted them enthusiastically. He had cool blue eyes and super-white teeth.

"I'm Leti. We're delighted you've come," he said, smiling brightly. "I'll be showing you around. It won't take long, and you're free to ask any questions. Follow me."

Sala stood uncertainly next to Cham. "Can I come?"

"You don't plan to sign up?" The way Leti said it, it sounded like an accusation.

Sala shook her head. "No. But I'd like to see. Please can I?"

Leti hesitated. "You're not supposed to, officially."

"Please," begged Cham. "I'd like her to come with me."

After a second, Leti agreed. "You can see some of it," he said. "But not all."

Maybe this man is hoping I'll change my mind, Sala thought.

Leti led them past the pods where they'd been swimming with dolphins, and then through some thick glass doors. Then there was another door. And another. Each time, Leti typed in a complicated code to let them in, as well as waiting by the recognition screen. *It's like a prison*, Sala thought.

They entered a huge laboratory.

"This is the test area," explained Leti. "After one month, new passengers will be brought here."

"Passengers?" Cham frowned.

"That's our name for everyone who signs up," said Leti. "You're going on a journey: an excursion to a new world. So the word 'passenger' describes you very well, don't you think?"

"I suppose so," agreed Cham.

"Good. So, as I was saying, your first month will be a trial. After that, you'll have two days of tests, to check that your body is behaving normally under pod conditions."

"Can he have visitors then?" Sala enquired eagerly.

"Of course. There will be a Contact Hour for visits each day."

Sala's heart fell. "Just an hour?"

Leti smiled, but the smile didn't reach his eyes. "We think it's quite generous," he said. "The tests will take most of the time available."

They moved on. Through an enormous glass wall, Leti showed them the energy storage area. It was extraordinary – a sea of complicated instruments and equipment.

"This is where we'll bring the passengers' energy," he explained. "Your body produces heat in the pod. We store that energy here."

Cham's parents asked a lot of questions, and Leti seemed to have an answer for everything. At last, when Dani and Tian had nothing more to ask, Leti smiled and spoke quietly to another technician, who was standing nearby. Then he turned to Sala. "I'm sorry, but you can't come any further with us. You've reached the limit of what I can show you. Only parents and close relations are allowed beyond this point, so Kaz here is going to take you back."

Sala touched Cham's hand with a sad smile, then followed Kaz back to the entrance. She waited there on the edge of her seat, anxious and impatient, as time passed. Fifteen, twenty minutes. She watched the hologram advertisement on the wall with its promises of a better future. *See the world*, smiled a beautiful woman. There was a grand ancient building on the banks of a river behind her.

Then that picture slowly disappeared, and a man took the woman's place. *Learn at the highest level*, he encouraged. The night sky appeared behind him, then the flames at the edge of a star. *Explore beyond Earth*. The star exploded slowly, throwing out a million rocks. Then the hologram changed again. Now it showed a robot working in a laboratory, its fingers like mechanical insects. *Dive inside the world of a cell*.

The voices of the people in the hologram were strange and slow, like voices in a dream. Sala stared. The hologram was pulling at her. It was like a tunnel, swallowing her up.

She forced herself to turn away. At last, Cham came back through the doors with Leti and his parents. He looked pale and tired, but a feverish excitement was burning in his eyes.

At last, Cham came back through the doors.

"So," Leti said, "we've been over everything now. Are you ready to sign?"

Cham looked at his parents. They hesitated. Then all three spoke at once. "Yes," they said.

Sala's heart almost stopped. Was that it? Decision made? No more discussion? Cham hadn't even looked at her. Maybe he didn't dare.

"Excellent," said Leti. "So now, just a few details. You're interested in the two-year program. Is that right?"

Cham cleared his throat. "That's right."

"Wage payments will be made to your family. Energy units must be saved for your own use. You will study, and choose various travel or sports experiences. You will also have one Ultranet Talk Hour per week to speak to friends and family. You will remain in the pod for this, so you will speak through your avatar."

One hour a week. That was all they had to make this separation less painful.

Leti continued. "After one month, as I've explained, you will be given tests. If your body is in good health, you will then return to the pod for a further twenty-three months."

He finished, and turned to Cham's parents, handing them a screen. "Because your son is still seventeen, we need your official agreement, please."

Cham's mom and dad took the screen, looking first at each other and then at Cham.

"Place your hand on the screen, one at a time," said Leti.

Cham's mom Dani went first. She lifted her hand. The screen was red, but as her skin touched it, it changed to orange, and then green. Tian followed.

"Now it's your turn," Leti said to Cham.

Cham moved stiffly forward, took the screen from his dad, and lifted his hand. Sala felt she was going to burst. Surely this wasn't really going to happen? But there was nothing she could do. She watched silently as the red light disappeared under Cham's hand. So simple. It turned to orange, and then green.

"That's it. Accepted," said Leti. "Passenger Cham, welcome to Pod Life. We look forward to seeing you in a week."

Sala's eyes filled with tears. A week. Just a single week. Then Cham would be torn away from her for two long years.

9

Wena

The week rushed by far too quickly. Sala spent every possible minute with Cham. They watched their favorite story-streams, and listened to their favorite music. They met with friends, especially Palo and Ding, who were entering the pods as well. Sala couldn't believe how much her life was suddenly changing, but she didn't try to discuss it with Cham. Pod Life was happening. That was it. What more could she say?

With just two days to go before Pod Life began, Sala woke up feeling depressed. She decided to go for a run at the energy center; maybe it would cheer her up. She arrived early and didn't have to wait in line, so in a few minutes, she was stretching her legs and then running mechanically, left-foot right-foot, on the machine.

She had been there for about thirty minutes when a woman began running on the machine next to her. Sala didn't look at her at first, but when the woman spoke, she recognized her voice at once.

"Don't look at me."

Sala jumped, and began to turn her head.

"I said *don't* look at me."

It was really difficult to obey. Sala kept on running, forcing herself to look straight ahead.

"When I leave, follow me," said the woman. "But not too closely. OK?"

Sala's thoughts flew to Cham – she was supposed to meet him in an hour. But this was really important. Since receiving Great-Uncle Eston's letter, Gran had been very quiet. She'd stopped gardening. Instead, she spent hours sitting on her bench in the Real Space, looking out over the city with a distant expression. Or she would suddenly tell them all one of her memories: of growing up with Eston or their suffering during the Oil Wars.

I have to do this. For Gran. For all of us, Sala thought. Maybe this would be the only opportunity to investigate.

After another ten minutes, the woman stepped off her machine. Sala stopped soon afterward, and, feeling guilty, she sent a message to Cham.

"I'm really sorry. I'm going to be late, but it's important. I'll explain. Love you." He would forgive her… and anyway, maybe she would come back with exciting news for everyone.

The woman left the energy center and Sala followed, keeping a safe distance. When she came toward the biggest walkway of all – the one that stretched right across the city – Sala's heart started beating faster. Was this a trap? Where were they going? But the woman didn't look back; she wasn't going to wait. It was now or never.

The walkway was busy. Determined not to lose sight of her guide, Sala pushed her way forward. The woman wore a bright yellow bag on her back, so at least she was easy enough to follow, but she walked rapidly, and Sala was soon breathless.

Before long, they passed through a district that Sala had never visited before. Here, the tower blocks seemed taller and more depressing than ever, built closely together so that the spaces between them were always in shadow. Up ahead, the woman took the next exit, and disappeared.

Sala felt fear catch hold of her. This was crazy; she shouldn't have come. But still, she followed. She left the walkway at the same exit, and looked around. Strange faces surrounded her;

everyone looked miserable and gray. She had lost sight of the woman – where had she gone? She tried to message Cham, but nothing happened. The ultranet was completely dead. *Sala, you're such a fool*, she thought. If the woman was leading her into a trap, she now had no way of contacting anyone.

But then she saw something yellow on the crowded street ahead: the woman's bag. Her guide was bending down, playing with her boot; and then she signaled with her fingers, inviting Sala on. Walking more slowly now, the woman went down a narrow passageway.

Sala felt like running away, but something made her keep going. *This is it*, she told herself.

Down the passageway. Through a side entrance into a tower block. Down a dark stairway with rough, slippery steps. Then… another door. It was open. Sala stepped into a room: an ordinary earth apartment, just like thousands of others.

In one corner, the woman was taking the yellow bag off her back. "Come in, come in," she said. "You're safe here."

"Am I? Why isn't my ultranet working?"

"We turned it off," said the woman. "To protect us all."

Sala's mouth dropped open. "You can just stop people's ultranet connections? How? Who are you?"

The woman smiled. She looked very different now that she was in her own surroundings – more friendly and unthreatening. Sala guessed she was about nineteen.

"My name is Wena. Come and sit," she said.

The room was almost empty. There were just two chairs, a simple metal table, and a very old sofa. Sala sat down on the sofa, and Wena sat next to her.

"What's this all about?" said Sala. "I want to know everything."

"I can't tell you *everything*," said Wena cautiously. "But I can say we're a rebellion. We're opposed to the government controlling everyone the way it does."

Sala looked around the room. "Are there many of you?"

"I can't tell you that."

"So, was that note really from Gran's brother? Are people alive out there – outside the city? How did you get the note across the force field?" She had so many questions.

"Yes, your grandmother's brother has been trying to contact her for a long time. And yes – there's a whole world out there. The government's story about contamination is all a big lie, but it's too dangerous to challenge it, or to talk about this."

"Why are you talking about it with me, then?" said Sala.

"We tested you first," said Wena. "We checked your ultranet history before giving you the rose fruit. We wanted to contact your grandmother directly, but she never goes out. So..." she hesitated, "we put a tiny bug inside the fruit. We needed to hear what she said. What you *all* said."

Sala's mind was racing. *If that's true, she knows all about us.* "So what *did* we say?" she demanded.

Wena smiled. "Your grandmother told you how she and her brother used the fruit to play tricks on people. Because it made them scratch."

Sala stared at her. She was absolutely right.

"The bug has stopped now. It only works for a short time," Wena carried on. "But we had to use it. We needed to be sure that you would be on our side. And that you wouldn't talk."

"We've been really careful!" said Sala. "The only person I've told is Cham."

"Yes. We've been checking him as far as possible, too."

"So you know he's going..."

"To do Pod Life? Yes, we know. It's a pity."

"Why?"

"We don't know enough about the pods yet. And we don't like it when the government develops new kinds of control."

"Control?" said Sala.

"Well, he can't leave the pod for two years, can he?" Wena's eyes were calm, but hard, too. "Like I said. Control."

Sala's heart beat a little faster. "So… why am I here?"

At that moment, a door opened at the far end of the room, and a man appeared. Behind him, Sala could just see a complicated collection of screens.

"Wena?" said the man. "Will you be long? I'd like a word."

"Ten minutes," said Wena.

"OK," he replied, and the door closed again.

"Who was he?" Sala asked curiously. "And what's in there?"

"That was Oban, our leader," said Wena. "And that's our control center. We're working on creating breaks in the force field, and blocking the wrist chips, too."

"You're joking!" breathed Sala. "That's unbelievable!"

"Believe it. For now, though, we want to help people like your grandmother. People who still have relations on the other side, and who might risk trying to leave."

"She'd *love* to leave!" said Sala. "But not without us," she added hurriedly. "Couldn't we all go?"

"In time, hopefully. Now, we're looking for people that the government is unlikely to miss. Like your grandmother, because she stays at home so much."

Sala took a deep breath, and tried to think clearly. "You've gotten people across?"

Wena shook her head. "Not yet. We're working on the force field. But we're getting close."

"So, how did Eston's note arrive?"

"A note is much easier than a person. We now have a secret agent, working within the government. She's able to cross the boundary."

Sala closed her eyes. For a moment, this felt as unreal as being in a pod. A different world. A new life. All the things that Gran had talked about. She opened her eyes, and Wena was still there, real and solid in front of her.

"So, what do you want me to do?"

"Talk to your grandmother. See if she would be prepared to take the risk. And apart from that, keep very, very quiet."

10

Sala's News

Sala half-wanted to rush home to tell Gran and Mom what had happened, but she didn't want to lose any of her remaining time with Cham. She was over an hour late for meeting him at the simulator center, and because her ultranet connection didn't come back on until she was almost there, she couldn't even call him or send him a message. So by the time she arrived, he looked desperately worried.

"Sala! What happened to you?" He wrapped his arms around her. "I've been going crazy."

"I'm sorry. I'm really, really sorry."

Cham kissed the top of her head. "It's OK. You're here now. But… where were you? Come on, I booked a space—"

"No!" Sala's mind was racing. She had to be so careful… Perhaps there were bugs in the simulator center. She'd never considered it before, when she'd had nothing to hide. But now it seemed an obvious place for the government to bug.

She dropped her voice. "Let's just walk."

Cham looked puzzled. "Well… all right, then."

They took the street that led toward the meat-growing laboratory. The whole way back from the earth apartment, Sala had been asking herself if it was OK to tell Cham about the rebellion. *Keep very, very quiet*, Wena had said. But Wena knew that Sala had told Cham about the rose fruit, didn't she? Anyway, Sala needed to tell Cham to try and persuade him not to go into a pod.

"So, come on, then," said Cham. "Where were you?"

"You have to promise to keep it a secret first."

"Another secret! You're full of them these days. I promise."

"It's that woman," Sala told him. "The one who brought the rose fruit. I met her again. She took me to an earth apartment and told me what they're doing."

"Who's 'they'?"

"She's part of a group. They've found out that it isn't true about the contamination. There's another world out there, Cham. They're trying to break down the force field and maybe help some people escape."

Cham's eyes grew wide with disbelief. "What?"

"It's true."

"Sala, I can't believe you took such a risk. I'm worried about you. You don't even know this woman and now she's filling your head with all these crazy stories..."

"It's not crazy. We have the letter from Gran's brother. And the rose fruit."

Cham shook his head. "Sala, please, listen to me. It's not real. It can't be real. I've been thinking about this. I know your gran is really excited, but... maybe they created that letter. Wrote it themselves. And the fruit – well, maybe they found it somewhere in the city. There must be an explanation."

"But why? Why would they do that? And how could they know that wild roses mean so much to Gran?"

"Maybe on the ultranet..." began Cham. Then he fell silent.

"Really? Come on, Cham. Think about it."

Cham reached for her hand. "I want to believe it," he said. "But it doesn't make sense to me. It just seems like a... a wild, crazy dream that they've invented to confuse you. Confuse *us*."

It was Sala's turn to fall silent. This world, the city with its wrist chips and simulators, was the only one they knew, but Gran often talked about life before the Oil Wars – how they used to walk freely in the forests, grow flowers and fruit, sing songs around fires on the beach, and travel to wonderful places. But none of Cham's grandparents were alive, so maybe it wasn't surprising that he found it hard to believe in another world.

"It *is* real, though," she said. "More real than Pod Life, Cham. The force field is real. The government is real. Our wrist chips are real. They control us. That's real. So if people are fighting it, secretly… why can't *that* be real?"

Cham looked uneasy. "Hey. You're giving me a hard time here, you know that?"

"Sorry. I don't mean to. I just wish…" Sala paused. Could she try to persuade him? Would he listen?

"Go on."

"I just wish you'd change your mind about Pod Life," she said, in a rush.

"Oh no…" Cham looked upset, and confused. "Please don't say that, Sala. You have to pay if you want to cancel. It's too late. And we've discussed it a million times. I love you. I'll still love you in two years. Then we'll be together. We can wait, can't we? If everything you say is true, we can do something about it then."

A little flame of hope lit up inside Sala. "You mean that?"

Cham pulled her closer. "Why not? By then, you'll be sure. You'll know what's going on."

"OK," said Sala slowly. "But you have to promise me. Promise me we'll investigate this more closely when you come out."

Cham kissed her. "Of course. With all my heart."

They walked back to the simulator center and spent an hour together alone in Space 29, where they chose their waterfall illusion. Then they met Niki, Palo, and Ding in a café for taste-pots. Cham and the other three talked excitedly about Pod Life, but Sala felt strange.

When they had talked about it before, she had felt left out; not jealous, exactly, because she was sure that she didn't want to join them. But different, separate, and kind of lonely. Now, that feeling had gone. Instead, she thought of Oban and Wena, and Gran's dreams about a life outside. She tried to imagine a future with no wrist chips and no force field. With gardens and forests and the ocean. Her secret burned fiercely inside her. She was dying to tell the others, but knew that she couldn't.

■ ■ ■ ■

By the time they had all said goodbye, and Sala had gotten home, evening had fallen. To her surprise, Gran wasn't in the kitchen preparing their meal as usual. Instead, Mom was busy cutting up Gran's vegetables from the Real Space.

"Hi, Mom! Where's Gran?"

"She's lying down, having a little rest."

"Why?" demanded Sala, alarmed. "Is she OK?"

"She'll be fine." Mom paused. "It's been hard for her, all this business about Uncle Eston. She's been hoping all week for more news. But I've been starting to wonder whether the whole thing was just a joke, or a trick, even."

"Well, it's not!" said Sala. "I have news, Mom. There's a group working against the government – a rebellion. They've discovered that the contamination is all a lie, and they're trying to find ways through the force field!"

Mom frowned. "Who told you this?"

"I saw the woman who gave us the fruit and the letter. She took me to their earth apartment—"

"Wait, wait!" said Mom. "Let's get Gran, then you can tell both of us."

Gently, they shook Gran awake. She looked exhausted at first; but the light came back into her eyes as Sala began to talk about her meeting with Wena.

"So, Gran, what do you think?" she asked breathlessly, when she'd finished her story.

"My goodness! It's wonderful," said Gran. "After all these years… someone is finally discovering the truth."

"But what about their suggestion?" asked Sala. "They want to help you leave. Would you go?"

Gran hesitated, for a long time. There were tears in her eyes. "Not without you," she said at last. "I couldn't possibly leave you all behind."

"But we'd follow!" said Sala eagerly. "You could go and live with Great-Uncle Eston. We could come later. Maybe when Cham comes out of the pod."

Gran shook her head. "Never again," she insisted. "Not after the Oil Wars. I never want to be separated from my closest family ever again. We all go, or none of us go."

It took a moment for her words to have an effect.

"Well, Gran," said Sala, "maybe one day, when Cham comes out of the pod, and they've managed to break through the force field, we really will be able to go together. What do you think about that, Mom?"

Mom hesitated. "Well… I have my job…"

"Oh, come on, now," said Gran. "You should know better than anyone that jobs in this city don't last. Even good ones like yours. And if, like Eston says, they really live freely in the outside world, you wouldn't want to stay here, would you?"

Mom nodded. "You're right. I would love to leave if I really believed we could. But we don't know that what this woman says is true – and nothing can happen right now anyway."

■ ■ ■ ■

Cham's last day was difficult for everyone. Sala wished she could see him on her own, but she knew that time with his family was precious. In the end, they had just an hour or two at his apartment before he left. Even then, they weren't alone.

"Make interface pictures for us, Cham," his two younger sisters begged. "Ones that talk with your voice. We want to have them beside our beds, so we can think of you every night."

Cham looked over at Sala apologetically. "Do you mind?" Then he turned to the girls. "We could do pictures of ghosts."

His youngest sister looked puzzled. "How?"

"Well, they'd be invisible. You'd have to imagine them."

Sala giggled. "He's just joking," she told the girls. "Come on. We'll all do some pictures together."

The girls were delighted, but inside, Sala felt like crying. Everyone tried to be happy and cheerful, but then it was all over. It was time to go.

The whole family went to the pod center, with Cham's mom telling his sisters to be brave, and his dad pale and quiet. The building seemed bigger than ever; the hologram wall seemed brighter. Sala watched as everyone gathered around Cham for their final goodbyes. Then she stepped forward, and wrapped her arms around him.

"Remember what we said," she whispered in his ear. "About the future."

"Don't worry," he whispered back. "I know you believe in something better than all this. I won't forget."

11

Ultranet Talk Hour

The first few days without Cham were horrible. It rained constantly, but Sala didn't really care; the dark, miserable skies matched her mood. She was counting the hours until she could speak to him again.

The only thing that made the time pass more quickly was her family's dream of the world outside. Sala went to the energy center every day, hoping she'd see Wena. Sometimes she took Apat with her, though he was less enthusiastic now that Cham couldn't go with them. He complained that Sala spent too long running, not realizing that she was waiting… and waiting… for something to happen.

And then, one day, it did. Apat was busy on the jumping machine, and Sala was collecting a drink from the café, when she heard a voice in her ear.

"Did you ask her?"

Sala raised her drink to her lips without looking at Wena. She knew the routine at last. "She wants to wait," she said. "Until we can all go."

"So, you were right." Wena sounded disappointed, and Sala risked a quick look at her. The other woman's expression was difficult to read. "But it's such a big opportunity. Maybe you could try again."

"I don't think she'll change her mind."

Wena was silent for a moment. "OK," she said at last. "We've talked enough. I have to go."

"Wait," said Sala hurriedly. "We support you – Gran is just not ready yet. But we'd love to know when you… you know, when you succeed."

"OK," said Wena quietly. She turned away, and before Sala could stop her, she picked up her yellow bag and disappeared through the center's doors.

What else could I say? Sala was kicking herself for not keeping Wena talking for longer. But she was so good at just melting away, disappearing before Sala had time to realize she was going. Now they had nothing. No fresh information. She'd just have to wait for Wena to appear again.

■ ■ ■ ■

The first week ended at last, bringing the day when Sala could speak to Cham again. Only three hours to go. Two hours. An hour. Thirty minutes. Sala engaged her virtual interface and sat waiting for him.

"Sala, it's me."

"Hey, passenger!" Sala was so excited. "How are you?"

"I'm fine," said Cham. His nose looked a little longer, and there was a different curve to his lips. Of course, Sala realized: this wasn't Cham. Now he was in the pod, it was only his avatar. But it was still wonderful to see this copy of him.

"What have you been doing?" she asked.

"Wow, Sala, I don't know where to start!" He sounded happy and enthusiastic. "OK, so, some things are boring. We have to learn all about the history of the government and things like that. I mean, yawn! But it's just a part of what we do. When we're not learning, we play sports, and they're all great…"

"Don't you ever rest?" Sala asked.

"Rest? There's no time. I'm learning to ski," said Cham. "After studying, I go to the Alps. Gorgeous mountains. Fantastic scenery. Perfectly white snow. I started on beginner areas – they're nice and easy to manage. Then when you get faster, you can try more difficult ones."

Cham went on and on, and Sala began to wonder when he would stop talking. He loved to talk when he was happy. She didn't mind that. But this long stream of words wouldn't stop flowing. It didn't seem quite right.

Now he was laughing. "I've fallen over loads of times," he confessed. "But it doesn't matter. I can't injure myself, so I get up and try again. I can't believe how fresh the air is and the sky is just..." At last, he paused for a second.

"Cham," said Sala.

Cham went on and on.

"Yeah, it's just this deep, deep blue—"

"Cham…" Sala hesitated. "It's not real, you know."

"I know." Cham sounded surprised.

"You're not *really* learning to ski."

"I didn't say I was."

"Well… not quite," said Sala cautiously. "Almost, though."

For the first time in their conversation, Cham was silent. Sala began to wonder if she'd offended him. Seconds passed.

"Sorry, I…" she started.

But Cham smiled. "It's OK. I'm boring you. How are you?"

"Oh! I'm fine. I really miss you, though." Sala wanted to tell him about seeing Wena, but she knew that she needed to be careful over the ultranet. She hesitated. "I saw that woman again."

"What woman?"

"*That* woman. The one who… who…"

"Oh. Her." Cham's voice suddenly sounded urgent. "Sala, I don't think you should see her anymore. It's… not good."

"But it's exciting, isn't it? I've only seen her once more. We're waiting for news."

"News of what?"

"I told you before. We have a plan, remember."

Cham's avatar looked uncomfortable. "Right. Well, please don't get involved with her."

Sala stared. She didn't know what to say.

"My mom and dad are waiting to speak to me," said Cham. "Sorry, Sala. I have to go."

"So soon?" Sala couldn't hide her disappointment.

"Yeah… I know."

"Well… never mind. Bye, Cham. I love you."

"Love you too, Sala."

And he was gone.

A whole week of waiting, and that was it. Over. Sala felt flat, and miserable. It wasn't enough. She wanted to touch him. She wanted to feel him close. What use was it, seeing an avatar? It wasn't even completely like him. His eyes were harder, and his smile seemed false. Not Cham. An illusion.

Worse than that, he seemed different. It wasn't just his avatar. His *character* seemed different. All that endless talk about his skiing… and then warning her about Wena and the rebellion. It bothered her.

She brought out her paints, and, sitting in her room, started working on a picture: the green leaves of Gran's Real Space, bright and bursting with life; gray tower blocks in the background. As she worked, she wondered why Cham didn't want her to talk to Wena. Maybe he was just being protective – worried that the rebels would put her in danger. It must be strange for him, not knowing where she was or what she was doing. *Next time, it will be fine*, she told herself.

"Sala! Are you there?" came Gran's voice from the kitchen.

"Coming!" Sala left her room and found that Gran had just prepared some fresh juice.

"There's not much," said Gran, handing Sala a little cup. "Not enough fruit to make more. I'm taking mine up to the Real Space. Coming?"

Sala followed Gran up the steps.

"Did you have a nice talk with Cham?" asked Gran.

"Well… yes… he's fine." Sala described how enthusiastic he'd been, but she didn't mention his warning. "I miss him terribly, Gran."

"Of course you do, my love," said Gran, a little absently. She was staring out at the view with that faraway look in her eyes – that look that Sala now recognized. Gran was thinking about her brother Eston.

"Gran… are you sure you're OK?"

"Oh, yes, don't mind me." But Gran was rubbing her back, where she'd been injured years ago. "I just wish I could do more. If I were stronger, I'd get out and join that rebellion."

"Would you?" Sala felt a little guilty. She'd been really excited to discover what the group was doing, but she hadn't considered actually *joining* them. Then she thought about Cham's warning, and felt confused. "It could be really dangerous, Gran."

"Of course," said Gran. "Most things worth fighting for involve a little danger. We all got involved, during the war. They trained us for it. But now… young people prefer to feel safe. And it's not surprising. That's how you've been taught to think."

Sala frowned. Gran's words bothered her. It wasn't like Gran to make her feel uncomfortable.

"I can try to contact them again, if you like."

"Oh dear, I didn't mean to suggest that," said Gran.

"But I could." Sala was feeling determined now. "You're right, Gran. This is our future, isn't it? There's no point in sitting back, just waiting for it to happen."

"I don't want you to take any risks," said Gran.

"No, no, I won't. I'll just see what I can find."

Gran smiled. "You take after me," she said. "I'm proud of you, Sala."

12

Looking for Answers

Sala would do it. She would find Wena, no matter what Cham had said. The next day, Sala started to look for her. She knew it would be best to go straight to the earth apartment, but she felt a little afraid to do that. She checked the energy center and the crowded walkways instead, but there was no sign of Wena. She wondered what to do. Did she dare go back to the earth apartment? What if Cham was warning her for a reason?

Don't be silly, she told herself. How could Cham know anything new about the rebels, living inside the pod? Anyway, Gran was right: it was worth it. *I'll be careful. I don't have to go inside… I can just wait for Wena or Oban to appear.*

She set off along the busy walkway, checking her ultranet connection as she went. Closer, closer to the strange district… Sala's ultranet stayed on. She took the same exit as before and walked cautiously toward the tower block. People were coming and going from the main entrance, like last time, but the narrow passageway down the side looked dark and empty. Sala watched and waited in the shadows. Nothing. No sign of Wena or Oban.

After an hour, her legs were aching from standing still. She should just go home… but curiosity was burning inside her. After looking around to check that no one was watching her, she slipped quietly down the passageway, and found the same door as before. It was open.

Sala checked her ultranet connection for the millionth time. It was still working. She took a deep breath and began to make her way down the stairway.

Everything was quiet. Every few steps, Sala stopped to listen. Down she went, into the depths of the tower block. The lights had been turned off; soon she was in complete darkness, so she turned on the lights on her virtual interface to guide her. At last, she reached the door to the earth apartment. She was about to knock, when she saw that this one wasn't closed either. She pushed it gently and, her knees trembling, she stepped into the room. There were no lights on. It was cold.

And there was no one there. The old sofa had been pushed against one wall, but there was no metal table or chairs.

"Wena!" she called, her voice high with fear. "Oban!"

No answer.

Sala rushed into the room that she had seen on her previous visit. It was deserted. All the screens had been taken away. The group had gone.

■ ■ ■ ■

"I don't understand it." Sala spoke in a low voice. She was at the kitchen table with Mom and Gran, but Apat was in his room, and she didn't want him to hear them.

"It *is* strange," agreed Gran. "But it reminds me of the war. Any kind of rebellion had to keep moving so that no one could discover it."

"So why hasn't Wena told me anything?" Sala rubbed her eyes. She was tired, and worried. She didn't know what to think anymore. "Cham doesn't even believe anything the rebels are telling us. Or he didn't, before he went into the pod."

Gran looked very surprised. "Why?" she said. "Didn't you tell him about Eston's letter?"

"Yes. But he says that it could be from anyone."

"Nonsense!" cried Gran. "I know Eston's handwriting."

"But… but it's so long since you last saw him, Gran," said Sala. "How can you be sure?"

Mom hadn't said anything yet. She she was looking thoughtful. "Cham has a point," she said slowly. "I know you've been very sure about the letter, Gran. It seems to say the right things, but… we don't have proof of anything."

At these words, Gran looked very downhearted. They all fell silent for a moment.

Then Mom spoke again. "Maybe we can find an answer. Can I take a look at the letter again?"

Gran brought out the note. Mom took it and inspected it closely, turning it over and over in her hands.

"I think I could test this," she said. "At work."

"Test it for what?" demanded Sala.

"There are fingerprints on the paper. That means there may be cells, too. If I find some, I can test them to see if they belong to someone in our family."

"That's a wonderful idea!" cried Gran. "But it's risky. What if you get caught?"

"I won't," said Mom. "I'll be careful. It might take a while to find the right time, but… I'll manage it."

It was good to know that they could do something to test Eston's letter; but even so, it wouldn't tell them where Wena and Oban's group had gone. With no Cham to talk to, and no news from Wena, the week went by very slowly for Sala.

She passed the time at the energy center, with Niki, or watching story-streams. But the day before her next Ultranet Talk Hour with Cham, she decided to go to the simulator center. Outside, the clouds looked gray and threatening, so she took the covered walkway. She dived onto it just as the rain began to pour, and started walking quickly.

She was almost at the simulator center exit when she saw something she recognized. A yellow bag.

"Wena," she breathed.

She raced along, trying not to bump into people, desperate to catch the young woman. Soon, she was almost level with her.

"Wena!" she called.

The woman turned, her green eyes shining with anger. "Are you crazy? Don't follow me!"

"I just… just… please, I need to talk to you."

The two of them were walking closely side by side now, and the walkway was moving fast. They passed the exit to the simulator center. Too bad: Sala would just have to come back the other way.

Wena wouldn't look at Sala. But then she spoke. "We did it."

"You… you got someone out?" gasped Sala.

"Yes. Just one. And then we had to move, before they came after us. Now leave me. Please don't follow me again."

Wena tried to hurry on, but Sala held onto her arm.

"Wait! Please, Wena! We want to help! And maybe when Gran hears this, it might change her mind."

Wena shook her off. "We think we may be able to get more people across. But please go now. If we need you, we'll find you."

Sala stopped walking, causing people behind to bump into her. She didn't care. She watched as Wena went on. Someone had escaped from the city… it was unbelievably exciting.

She rushed home with the news and found Gran in the Real Space.

"They did it!" Gran cried, clapping her hands in delight.

"Do you think we can believe it?" asked Sala.

"I don't see why not," said Gran. "Why would they lie to you? If they've had to move their whole organization, it seems quite likely that they've managed something big."

"I hope so…" Sala heard the door of the apartment open downstairs, and frowned. Mom usually got home much later than this, and Apat was at school.

"Mom! Is that you?" she called.

"Yes! Everyone, come here!"

Sala and Gran hurried down from the Real Space.

"Mom, what is it?" asked Sala. "Is everything OK?"

Mom smiled. "Everything is fine."

"You've tested the fingerprints on Eston's letter?" asked Gran eagerly.

"Yes!" Mom fished it out of her bag, her eyes bright with success. "I found cells from six different people. Myself, of course. You, Gran, and Sala – because we all touched it. Two people we don't know. And… another family member. Not one of us – I tested, to be sure. So it has to be a very close relation!"

"Which means it must be Eston!" Gran gasped. "That's absolutely wonderful!"

The three of them did a dance around their tiny living room. The rebellion was real. Great-Uncle Eston was real! And maybe, one day, they would be able to meet him.

For a few hours, celebrating with her family, Sala felt full of hope. The future was bright. When she saw the real Cham again at the end of the month, she would persuade him to leave Pod Life behind. He would see the truth, and together they'd start a whole new adventure…

Great-Uncle Eston was real!

13

Not the Same Person

The following morning, Sala got up early for the big event of her week: Cham's Ultranet Talk Hour.

"Hi, Cham!" Sala waved at his avatar eagerly. It was so wonderful to see his face again. "How's it going?"

"Hey, Sala," he said. "Greetings from the Alps!"

"You're still there?"

"Yeah. During my free time," said Cham. "Ding has joined me there, too. We've been having a lot of fun! This week, they gave us the chance to try snowboarding as well as skiing."

Sala imagined Cham and Ding in their strange virtual life. "Sounds great. Lucky Ding, being there with you!"

"Hey, you're not jealous, are you?"

"N-noo…"

"Yes, you are," said Cham cheerfully. "Don't blame you, to be honest. Life here is sweet, Sala. Two years are going to fly past. You know, I'm starting to think I might stay in for a while longer."

He said it so lightly that Sala wasn't sure she'd heard right.

"Sorry? You don't mean that, do you?"

Cham laughed apologetically. "Well, you know, it's great in here. You should seriously think about joining me."

"Cham… please don't say that." Sala swallowed. "Please don't joke with me. We have plans, remember?"

"Plans?" Cham's avatar looked confused.

"Cham! Don't you remember the woman?" she demanded. She paused. She was desperate to let him know the exciting news. "I met her on the walkway. They're doing really well.

And Mom has checked the fingerprints on the letter. We know it's real."

"What letter?"

Sala couldn't believe it. How had he forgotten?

"The letter from Gran's brother." The words slipped out before she could stop herself, and she knew at once that she shouldn't have said it. What if the government was bugging their conversation?

"Ah... that! I remember now," he said. Then his face clouded over. "But Sala... you're not planning anything with that woman, are you? They teach us to report things like that."

Report it? Sala's stomach turned to ice. "Cham, what are you talking about?"

"It's just common sense. We have to report anything we think is strange. That's what makes the world safe."

Sala was horrified. Where was Cham, the real Cham? She had to invent something fast. "Cham, you're talking such nonsense," she said, laughing. "What's strange about a letter? I'm talking about the one Mom found under her bed."

Cham looked more confused than ever. "Under the *bed*?"

"Yes. She found an old letter under the bed."

"Oh. Well, I guess that's OK," said Cham. There was a silence. "But there was another letter, wasn't there?"

"That was nothing," said Sala hurriedly. "We threw it away."

"Glad to hear it," said Cham. "Wise move. So, what do you think? How about coming to join me?"

"I'll think about it," said Sala, suddenly afraid of what else he might say.

"You will?" Cham sounded pleased. "That's so cool. It would make everything much, much easier, wouldn't it?"

It was all wrong. Sala was certain now. Something had

happened to Cham. He was changing. The pod was changing him. Terrified, Sala rushed from her room as soon as she and Cham had finished talking.

"Mom! Gran!" she shouted.

"Sala! What on earth is it?" Mom called down from the Real Space. "We're up here."

Sala ran up the steps so fast she almost tripped. "It's Cham. We have to get him out. He's changing! The pod is having some kind of effect on him!" she gasped.

"Hey, hey," said Mom gently. "It can't be that bad. Slow down. Explain properly."

Gran and Mom listened as Sala described the conversation. "It's horrible. He's not the same person anymore," she finished, bursting into tears. "After just two weeks!"

Gran and Mom listened.

"All right, all right," said Gran gently. "It's worrying, I agree. But let's try to stay calm." She looked at Sala's mom. "What do you think? Could the pod be doing something to him? Changing the way he thinks somehow?"

"It certainly sounds like it. Anything is possible."

"So what can we *do*?" Sala cried. "We have to get him out!"

Gran and Mom fell silent. Sala walked in circles around the tiny Real Space, trying to think of a way forward.

"He comes out for tests in a couple of weeks, doesn't he?" said Mom. "You can try to talk to him then."

"What about his family?" asked Sala. "I'm not sure he'll agree to leave the pod anyway, but if he does, they might still want him to stay. They'd lose a lot of money if he comes out."

"That's true. But maybe they've noticed he's different, too," said Gran. "They know him better than anyone. Maybe they're worrying about the effect on him already."

Hope lit up inside Sala. Of course, they would have seen that Cham had changed! And they'd permit him to leave the pod at once if they thought it was damaging him.

"I'm going over there," said Sala. "I have to talk to them. Right now."

■ ■ ■ ■

It was strange, going to Cham's apartment and knowing Cham wouldn't be there. Sala stood by the recognition screen and waited until Cham's mom Dani came to the door.

"How lovely to see you, Sala," said Dani. "Come in!"

The whole family was there – Cham's parents and both his sisters. They gave her a big welcome, and Dani made green tea. Then they sat around the kitchen table, looking expectantly at Sala. Now that she was here, how was she going to say what she needed to?

"It was good to talk to Cham just now, wasn't it?" said Dani.

"Mmmm," said Sala, looking down at her tea.

"He's having lots of fun," said one of his sisters. "He's learning to ski! I wish we could join him. It's not fair that we have to stay here."

None of them seemed at all alarmed or worried about Cham.

"I think your mom and dad would miss you," Sala said to his sister. "And…" She paused, then forced herself to be brave. "I'm not sure that Pod Life is all that good, you know." She looked over at Cham's parents. "Does Cham seem… normal to you?"

"Oh, he's having a wonderful time," said Dani. "I'm so glad he's enjoying it."

"But – don't you think he seems… different?" asked Sala desperately.

Cham's parents looked puzzled. "In what way?"

Sala bit her lip. She couldn't tell them about Gran's letter, or the meetings with Wena. "He… he said he might want to stay in the pod, after the two years," she said. "It really worried me. He shouldn't be enjoying it *that* much, should he?"

"Oh, Sala!" said Dani, in a bright, sincere voice. "Don't you worry. I'm sure he didn't mean it. It's all new and exciting right now, but he'll get tired of it. After two years, he'll be dying to see you and the real world again!"

I'm going to have to be blunt, thought Sala. "Look, I know this will sound strange, but to me, he doesn't seem the same," she insisted. "I think the pod is like a drug. It's doing something to his mind."

Everyone looked rather shocked, and uncomfortable.

Tian cleared his throat. "That's quite a thing to say, Sala."

"I know—"

"You're doubting what the government is doing." There was a warning in Tian's voice now. "Of course you miss him. We all do. But I believe that this is best for all of us." He looked over at Dani, who nodded in agreement. "We both believe that. So please, be careful what you say."

Sala stared at them. They didn't see the problem at all.

"We're so grateful to him," said Dani, in a dreamy voice. "When he comes out, we'll be able to move to a sky apartment. It will be so nice to leave here."

Hopeless. Completely hopeless, Sala thought as she sat finishing her green tea. There was only one thing she could do. She would have to persuade Cham to leave by herself. Maybe his parents would be disappointed, but it was the only responsible thing to do; they'd thank her, in the end.

■ ■ ■ ■

There was one last Ultranet Talk Hour with Cham before the end of the month, but Sala decided it wasn't even worth trying to talk to him about leaving. She didn't want any more warnings, any more threats. She needed to see the real Cham, not his avatar. The time came and went. Cham had a new virtual hobby now – riding – and he talked happily about going out on horses and competing in races with Ding and Palo. But to Sala, his voice seemed high and feverish. He didn't ask her many questions; and although his avatar was looking at her, his eyes were glassy and unseeing.

When the ultranet interface went dead, she sat quietly for a moment. So much had changed in just a few short weeks. On the one hand, she could now see a future full of possibilities... but on the other, her life with Cham had never felt more uncertain.

14

Contact Hour

"**P**arents! Friends!" called a loud voice. "Please line up this way…"

Cham's test days had arrived at last, and Sala had joined Dani, Tian, and Cham's two sisters at the pod center for their first Contact Hour with him. The line moved forward slowly; then a technician called Odem led them through the thick glass doors, past the test laboratory, and into a waiting room. Other people were already there, sitting around circular tables.

"We will bring Cham here to you," said Odem.

Sala looked around at all these people. It was going to be difficult to talk to Cham privately. She wasn't even sure if his family would give them time alone together – but she'd have to make sure it happened. Somehow.

And then… there he was, in the doorway. He looked pale and confused, but it was him. The real Cham. Not an avatar. *Cham.* But after the conversation where he'd talked about reporting things, Sala felt unsure of him, all the same.

Dani rushed over and threw her arms around him. "Cham! Oh! It's *you*! Come, come – we're all over here…"

She led him to the table. Cham followed, but his steps seemed heavy and slow. Anxiety grew in Sala's stomach. *He's still not the same. He's like a sleepwalker.* She watched as the whole family greeted him. He laughed and smiled and seemed happy to see them all; but to Sala, he was different. What was it? She wasn't sure. Just something… dead… in his eyes. Even when he took her in his arms, it didn't feel quite the same.

The minutes passed. Cham told them all about skiing,

snowboarding, riding a horse.

"What about your studies?" asked his mom.

"Oh, yeah. They're OK. We learn a lot about how the government looks after us. They make you realize how lucky we are. The pods are a great invention," he said, in a strangely mechanical voice.

Dani smiled. "That's good. I'm sure you'll learn so many interesting things," she said encouragingly.

Sala stared at her in disbelief. She wanted to scream at his parents. *Don't you see? Can't you see? This isn't Cham!*

She took a deep breath. "Actually, I'd really like to talk to Cham about his studies," she said. "Do you think we could have a few minutes to talk on our own, at the end of the hour?"

Cham's parents looked at each other. "Well… I should think so…" said Tian. He laughed. "To talk about studies, is it? Very likely, you two love-birds."

Sala gave a fixed smile. She didn't care what he thought. Right now, all she wanted was to talk to Cham. She kept on smiling as Cham showed his little sisters where his body was connected to the pod.

"Does it hurt?" asked the youngest.

"Not at all," said Cham. "It's just like this."

His sisters giggled as he ran his fingers over their heads. Sala watched impatiently. Normally she loved it when Cham was fooling around with his sisters, but now she thought she'd explode.

Fifteen minutes left. Would they ever leave?

Twelve minutes. Ten… Dani and Tian stood up.

"Come on, girls," said Tian. "Let's give Sala a few minutes alone with Cham."

There were hugs and goodbyes. The girls cried, and Cham

kissed everyone. Then, at last, they were alone.

Five precious minutes left.

"Cham." Sala held his hand. "I've missed you so much."

Cham smiled his lovely warm smile. "Yes. Me too. How is everything? Your mom and gran? Is Apat behaving himself?"

Sala was surprised. She felt a rush of delight. So the real Cham was still there, underneath! Maybe he'd just needed a little time to get used to them all again…

"Oh yes," she whispered. "And we have news."

"Really? Tell me." Cham moved a little closer. "I hope they're all OK."

He seemed like the old Cham: thoughtful, kind. This might be easier than she'd imagined. She had to try. She just had to hope that no one was listening in on their conversation.

"Listen, Cham. We have proof. We know that the letter really came from Gran's brother. My mom proved it in the laboratory. So we really believe now that there's a better life out there. If you come out of the pod, we can try and find it together. Please. I need you to come out."

Cham went very still. As Sala held her breath, his eyes slowly hardened. "I was afraid you'd say something like that."

"But Cham… We could have a different future. A real one."

"No, Sala." Cham looked sad, even disappointed. "These people are dangerous. They're filling your head with lies. I tried to warn you before."

"But it's *real*."

"I want to protect you."

"But how—"

"You have to join us in the pods. If you're in here, I'll know they can't reach you," he said. "If you don't, I'll have to report all this. It's my duty, Sala. I have to keep you safe."

A bell rang; the hour was over. Technicians appeared at the door and everyone began to stand up.

Sala was in shock. "You don't mean it?" she begged Cham.

For a second, Cham looked apologetic. "I can't help it," he said. Then his expression hardened again. "Think about it and tell me tomorrow." He paused. "It's only because I love you, you know."

"You don't mean it?"
Sala begged Cham.

■ ■ ■ ■ ■

Sala played with the plate of food in front of her; she couldn't eat a thing.

"So he says it's for your own protection," said Gran bitterly.

"But how have they persuaded him to think like that?" asked Sala. "I mean… they're teaching him all about obedience and how wonderful the government is. But why has he listened?"

"It's not his fault," said Mom quietly. "It seems that the pod is designed to change the way people think. It's hard to fight that kind of influence. Don't blame him, Sala."

"That's right," agreed Gran. "It's really difficult. During the Oil Wars, they had to train us how to keep our minds strong, in case we were caught by people who wanted to change the way we thought."

"I'm not blaming him," said Sala miserably. "I just don't understand. And I don't know what to do."

Silence fell. Mom got up and gathered the dinner plates. "Let's think about this reasonably. Cham doesn't know much about the rebellion, does he?" she said. "So there's not much he can report."

"But he knows about the letter from Eston," said Gran. "So if he tells them about that, they will investigate. They'll come here."

"No!" Sala gasped, horrified. "We can't let that happen!"

The door of the apartment opened and Apat came in, back from visiting a friend for dinner.

"What's wrong?" he demanded at once, looking around at their troubled faces.

"Nothing, nothing," said Gran.

Sala smiled at her little brother, thinking how innocent he looked. It was too risky to let him know all their secrets. If the government came asking them questions, it would be better, for now, that he knew nothing at all.

Once Apat was in bed, Gran, Mom, and Sala talked long into the night, discussing Cham's threat.

"If the government comes here, they won't find anything," said Gran. "I'll make sure of it."

"Of course they won't," said Mom. "But the problem is, they can test Cham to check if he's lying. They will soon discover he's telling the truth – that as far as he knows, we *did* receive a letter. They'll make us tell them everything we know."

It was a horrible thought. Everyone knew that the government had cruel and terrible ways of forcing people to speak. Sala couldn't imagine anything worse in the whole world than someone trying to harm Gran, Mom, or Apat.

"I'm so sorry I told him," she said guiltily.

"It's not your fault, Sala," said Gran. "It's not Cham's fault, either. He is completely innocent. We must remember that."

"I know… but…" Sala hung her head.

There had to be an answer. There *had* to be!

"Do you think the rebels would hide us?" asked Mom. "If we can find them again, that is. Then maybe they would help us escape across the boundary."

"But… that would mean leaving Cham behind forever." Sala's eyes filled with tears. "I know what he's doing is awful, but I still love him, Mom."

"Anyway, we don't have a clue where the rebels are," said Gran. "Wena didn't tell you, did she?"

Sala shook her head. Their hopes and dreams seemed to be in ruins. It was clear to them now: the pods were just another way of controlling everyone. Young people who did it would stop thinking independently. When they came out, they would be obedient servants of the government.

Sala's tears began to flow. Gran held her hand and Mom put an arm around her shoulders. She missed the real Cham so much. She thought about all the wonderful times they'd had together. It had been so much fun, in spite of their lives being so limited. Cham was such a good person – warm and kind and funny. If he hadn't been so generous, buying her that pod experience, none of this would have happened.

They went to bed at last, but Sala couldn't sleep. She thought of everything that she, Mom, and Gran had talked about over and over. And then, just before daybreak, she had an idea. She got up and found Gran in the kitchen, drinking fruit tea.

"You couldn't sleep either?" Gran asked.

Sala shook her head.

"Let me make you some tea."

Sala watched as Gran boiled the water. "Gran," she said, "you remember what you said last night, about the Oil Wars? You said… they taught you how to protect your mind. You know – against people who wanted to change the way you thought."

Gran put Sala's tea in front of her. "Yes. We were given exercises to practice, so that if we were caught, we could stay strong." She looked at Sala's face.

Sala drank some of the hot, fruity tea, and felt her idea growing stronger. "Could you teach them to me?" she asked.

Gran gave her a long, hard stare. There was a moment's silence. Then she nodded slowly.

15

Coming In

At the pod center the next day, Sala sat in the shadow of the huge hologram, waiting. She felt sick. Cham's parents and sisters sat next to her, talking quietly, but she didn't join in. She was saving all her strength for when they saw Cham.

"We're ready for visitors!" called a cheerful voice. It was Zee, who had guided Cham and Sala through their dolphin experience. Sala stood up. Her knees were trembling, but along with Cham's family, she followed Zee through the glass doors.

Zee took them to the same room as before. One by one, the pod passengers appeared to greet their families and friends. Sala watched them, searching their faces for clues. Some of them looked a little stiff and strange, maybe; but most of them seemed perfectly normal. And the way they were smiling, none of the other parents seemed to suspect that anything was wrong.

At the far end of the room, she saw Ding, and waved. Then Dani's voice broke into her thoughts. "Sala! Cham is here!"

Sala forced herself to smile as Cham came over and hugged everyone. *Look happy. Look normal*, she told herself. Cham sat down and looked at the pictures that his sisters had drawn for him, then answered his parents' questions about the tests.

"Are they happy with the results?" asked Tian.

"Yeah. I'm still in perfect health!" said Cham. "Pod Life seems to suit me. It's not doing me any harm at all."

"Oh, that's so good to know," said Dani.

"Well, I can recommend it," said Cham, looking straight at Sala. What was that look in his eyes? A challenge, or just a question? Whichever it was, Sala knew the moment had come.

"Actually, I've got something to tell you all," she said slowly. "I had a long discussion with Mom and Gran last night." She paused. This was hard. Really hard. *Look happy. Look normal.* She tried to seem excited. "Cham is having such a good time that we've decided I should do Pod Life, too."

She met Cham's eyes. Did he suspect her reasons? She desperately hoped not. As a huge smile of delight spread over his face, she felt suddenly weak all over.

"When?" Cham demanded breathlessly. "*When?*"

"Not immediately," said Sala. "But soon. In a week."

"Oh! That's fantastic!" Cham got out of his chair and hugged her, burying his face in her hair. "You don't know how much this means to me."

Sala swallowed. It was wonderful to feel his arms around her again. She closed her eyes, and let herself enjoy it, just for this moment. It might be the last real moment with him she'd have.

■ ■ ■ ■

The slippery, silvery suit felt cool. Underneath it, metal, rubber, and plastic attachments lay on the surface of her skin. Her whole body was connected now. Sala waited in the pod as they made the final checks, bright lights blinding her from above.

She closed her eyes. *Mom, Gran, Apat.* For one last time, she thought of them. With her new strength of mind, she didn't think about the tears and hugs as she'd said goodbye. Instead, she imagined them standing in a beautiful garden, surrounded by greenery, with wild roses nodding gently nearby. This, Gran had taught her, was what she must think of.

She thought of Gran's final advice. *Awareness is the greatest weapon you have. When you know what they're trying to do, you're one step ahead; you've won half the battle already. If they can't surprise you, it's harder for them to control you.*

"Final attachment."

"Check."

"Energy connections tested."

"Check."

Sala forced her mind to go still; the voices seemed to come from far away. She did not belong in the pod. She did not belong to the government. She would not be their tool, used like Cham to pull other people in. She was Sala, only Sala. And somehow, she hoped, she would reach Cham, through his avatar, and find the real person inside once more. *We'll beat them*, she told herself. *We'll win.*

"Pod closure."

There was a low mechanical noise as the walls of the pod began to shut softly around her.

This is it, Cham. I'm coming in.

avatar *(n)*   something that looks like you, but is not you, often on a computer screen, e.g. the picture of you when you are playing a computer game

beep *(n & v)*   a short, high noise

boundary *(n)*   a real or imagined line that marks where one area of land ends and another begins

bug *(n & v)*   a small piece of equipment with a microphone used for secretly listening to what people are saying

cell *(n)*   the smallest living part of an animal or a plant

chip *(n)*   a very small piece of a computer

click *(n)*   a short, sharp sound

code *(n)*   a group of numbers or letters that you need in order to open a lock or door

contaminate *(v)*   to make something dirty or poisonous; **contaminated** *(adj)*; **contamination** *(n)*

dolphin *(n)*   an intelligent animal that lives in the ocean, breathes air, and looks like a large, smooth, gray fish

energy *(n)*   We get this from electricity, gas, etc., and it is used to make machines work and to make heat and light; the ability to be very active without becoming tired

engage *(v)*   to move a piece of a machine or equipment into place so that it works

exercise *(v & n)*   to move or use your body, or part of your body, to keep it strong and well

fingerprint *(n)*   a mark that a finger leaves when it touches something

flash *(v)*   to shine brightly for a very short time, or to shine on and off again very quickly

giggle *(v)*   to laugh in an excited or silly way

gorgeous *(adj)*   very pleasant or attractive

hologram *(n)*   a special kind of picture which appears to be 3D or solid, especially one created using light

hug *(v & n)* to put your arms around somebody to show your love or friendship; to hold something close to your chest

illusion *(n)* something that your eyes tell you is there or is true, but in fact is not

interface *(n)* a device, e.g. a screen, which someone uses in order to communicate with a computer

laboratory *(n)* a special room or building where scientists work

nanobot *(n)* an extremely small robot

nod *(v)* to move your head down and up again quickly, usually because you agree with or understand something

opportunity *(n)* a chance to do something, often something good or that you want to do

pod *(n)* a very small and simple building or room, often round in shape

robot *(n)* a machine that can do work by itself, often work that humans do

set off *(v)* to leave on a trip or start going somewhere

simulation *(n)* a situation that seems real but is created by a computer; **simulator** *(n)* a piece of equipment that produces a simulation

ski *(v)* to move over snow on skis (long, thin objects that you fasten to your boots) as a sport; **skiing** *(n)*

snowboarding *(n)* a sport like skiing where your boots are fastened to a board instead of skis

space *(n)* an area for a particular purpose; the empty place between things

splash *(v & n)* If liquid splashes, it moves or hits something or someone noisily.

store *(v)* to keep something to use later; **storage** *(n)*

strength *(n)* how strong or powerful you are, either in your body or in your mind

technician *(n)* a person with special training who works with machines or instruments

trust *(v)* to believe that somebody is honest and good and will not hurt you in any way

ultranet *(n)* *(an invented word in this story)* a large group of connected computers used for communicating, very similar to today's internet

unit *(n)* what we use to measure something, e.g. a centimeter is a unit of length

virtual *(adj)* used to describe something that is done or seen using computers; **virtually** *(adv)*

waterfall *(n)* a place where a river falls from a high place to a low place

The growing world of virtual reality

The story happens in the future, in a world that has been deeply changed by war. The government in that world uses virtual reality (VR) – simulations – to amuse and control its people. But how close are we to having a similar level of VR in our society? We may be much closer than you would think. That could be exciting, but is VR always a good thing?

Levels of virtual reality

Specialists in virtual reality measure different experiences by how "immersive" they are. A truly immersive VR experience is one that completely persuades your mind that you are doing or seeing something real. So in the story, the pods are completely immersive; the simulators are still immersive, but less so.

In today's world, playing VR computer games and watching 3D movies are the most immersive virtual experiences that most people are likely to have – for now. But there are also more specialist uses for VR technology, and these are developing all the time. Here are some examples:

- Pilots are taught to fly using flight simulators.
- Some museums offer virtual tours on the internet, so that you can see inside without needing to visit.
- Doctors can practice operations using virtual reality.

Good or bad?

Figures show that young people around the world are spending more and more time experiencing virtual worlds, most commonly by playing computer games. In the future, it is likely that people will spend much more time studying, communicating, and working virtually, too. But more time spent in a virtual world means less time spent in the real world:

- Less time face to face with friends and family
- Less time exploring the world around you
- Less time playing sports or enjoying nature

The question is: if you can experience all these things virtually, does it matter?

RESEARCH Read "Beyond the Story" and research the answers to these questions.

1 What other specialist uses are there for VR technology today? Find two more examples.

2 What is "augmented reality"?

---

operation (*n*)   when a doctor cuts into somebody's body to take out or repair a part inside

specialist (*adj & n*)   knowing a lot about something particular

Think Ahead

1 Read about the story on the back cover, and look at the chapter titles. How much do you know about the story? Check (✓) the true sentences.

   1 It is a story about an imagined future world. ☐

   2 Sala and Cham travel a lot. ☐

   3 Sala has only just met Cham. ☐

   4 Sala and Cham have to make some important decisions. ☐

2 What do you think is going to happen at the end of the story? Choose one answer.

   1 Cham and Sala can't agree what to do, so they separate.

   2 Sala decides that she has to join Cham in his new life.

   3 Everyone in the city is given the chance for a new future.

   4 Sala and her family decide to leave the city.

3 **RESEARCH** Before you read, find the answers to these questions.

   1 Scientists say that the world's oil will all be used by some time in the future. How long do they think our oil will last? You will probably find differing opinions. What might change how long it lasts?

   2 How many people are there on the Earth at the moment? Studies show that this number is going up all the time. How many people will there be in fifty years?

Chapter Check

FOREWORD & CHAPTER 1 Put the events in order.

a Sala and her friends sat in a virtual park.

b Cham gave Sala the gift of a pod experience.

c The ten-year Oil Wars ended.

d Sala and Niki walked past the meat-growing laboratory.

e Sala and Niki reached the simulator center.

f The land around the city became contaminated.

g Cham and Sala started going out with each other.

CHAPTERS 2 & 3 Choose the correct answers.

1 After Sala and Cham left the simulator center, …
   a a stranger stopped Sala in the street.
   b a friend said hello to Sala in the street.

2 Gran's back often hurt because she…
   a had been injured in the Oil Wars.
   b did too much work in the garden.

3 Wild rose plants…
   a were Sala's great-uncle's favorite plant.
   b used to grow beyond the city boundary.

4 People used the energy center a lot because it…
   a offered both exercise and extra energy units.
   b was very cheap to get in.

5 Sala was upset with Cham for…
   a arriving too early at the energy center.
   b thinking about doing Pod Life without telling her.

6 How was Cham's life different from Sala's?
   a He was studying to be a worker in the simulator center.
   b His family was poorer and lived underground.

CHAPTERS 4 & 5 Are the sentences true or false?

1 Cham's apartment had a hologram wall.

2 Sala and Cham had another argument.

3 It wasn't possible for Cham's dad to do Pod Life because there was an age limit.

4 Sala said she would think about doing Pod Life.

5 Sala did not feel at all worried about the dolphin pod experience.

6 Sala and Cham had to wear red suits.

7 Cham really enjoyed the experience of swimming with the dolphins.

8 When she left the pod, Sala laughed.

CHAPTERS 6 & 7 Match the sentence halves.

1 Zee…

2 Cham…

3 Sala's mom…

4 Cham's father…

5 The strange woman…

6 Gran's brother…

a wrote about a good life beyond the city.

b brought some high-energy drinks.

c handed Sala a note to give to Gran.

d was quiet on the way home.

e got some good quality meat from work.

f had no more work.

CHAPTERS 8 & 9 Choose the correct words.

1 Sala's mom said not to trust Cham's *parents* / *cousins*.

2 Sala told Cham that the government had lied about the *simulation* / *contamination* beyond the city boundary.

3 Sala thought the pod center was like a *palace* / *prison*.

4 Cham and his parents had to place their hands on a *screen* / *window* to accept the Pod Life agreement.

5 When Sala followed the strange woman, she thought it might be a *trap* / *game*.

6 Wena had checked Sala's ultranet *connection* / *history* before she gave her the wild rose fruit.

7 There had been a *chip* / *bug* hidden inside the rose fruit.

8 The rebels were trying to get through the *force field* / *control center*.

CHAPTERS 10 & 11 Are the sentences true or false?

1 Sala apologized to Cham for being very late.

2 Cham believed what Sala told him about the rebels.

3 Gran said that she didn't want to leave her family.

4 Cham's family and Sala said goodbye to Cham at the pod center.

5 Cham talked a lot about climbing in the mountains.

6 Sala told Cham about meeting her friend Niki.

7 Sala thought that Cham's character seemed different.

8 Gran said she had received training during the war.

CHAPTERS 12 & 13 Replace the <u>underlined</u> words with the words below.

angry   bed   find   report   riding   test

1 Sala decided that she was going to <u>warn</u> Wena.

2 Sala's mom said she would <u>destroy</u> Great-Uncle Eston's letter.

3 Wena seemed <u>happy</u> when she saw Sala in the street.

4 Cham said he should <u>keep</u> the letter.

5 Sala lied and said that Mom had found the letter under her <u>bag</u>.

6 Cham's new virtual hobby was <u>tennis</u>, which he did with Ding and Palo.

CHAPTERS 14 & 15 Choose the correct answers.

1 In the Contact Hour, Sala thought Cham looked like he was…
   a sleepwalking.   b feeling ill.

2 Cham said Sala should join him in the pods so he could…
   a show her important things.   b protect her.

3 Gran and Mom agreed that the government must be…
   a making Cham sick.   b trying to influence Cham.

4 Sala asked Gran to teach her…
   a how to protect her mind.   b all about the Oil Wars.

5 The tests showed that Cham…
   a was in good health.   b had become a little weak.

6 Sala told Cham that she had decided to…
   a help Gran escape across the city boundary.
   b join him in doing Pod Life.

Focus on Vocabulary

1 **Complete the sentences with the correct words.**

avatar   illusion   laboratory   technician

1 Sala's mom worked at a _____.
2 Cham's _____ did not seem like the real him.
3 Zee was a _____ at the pod center.
4 In the simulator center, you could choose to watch an _____ of a park.

2 **Read the clues and complete the word puzzle.**

Down
1 a word for someone you find really beautiful
2 what happens when something lands suddenly in water

Across
3 a place where a river suddenly drops down
4 a short, high sound
5 to wrap your arms around another person

Focus on Language

1 **Complete the sentences from the story with *must have,
 can't have, should,* or *shouldn't have.***

1 Sala felt fear catch hold of her. This was crazy; she
 _____ come.

2 You're the one with doubts about it, so you _____
 decide. I would do it – but only if you want to do it, too.

3 There's nowhere in the city for wild roses to grow. But of
 course it _____ come in from outside… unless…

4 A woman gave it to me. … I think she _____
 followed me.

2 **DECODE** **Read the extract. Then answer the questions.**

"My mom is really upset," Cham carried on. "And the thing is…"
 He stopped[1], and Sala realized what he was going to say.
 "Pod Life," she said. "Cham, no!"
 "Tell me, then!" he demanded. "Tell me what else I should do."
 "But I'd really miss you – and so would your family…"
 "I'll be doing it *for* my family," Cham pointed out. "You can
see that, can't you?'
 Sala nodded[2]. "Yes. Yes. Sorry."

1 Underline three words or phrases that can be replaced with
 "said".

2 Which of the underlined words or phrases shows that…
 a Cham is speaking in a strong voice?
 b Cham wants Sala to understand something?
 c Cham has already been talking?

3 Look at words 1 and 2. Why does Cham stop? What does Sala
 show by nodding?

Discussion

1 Read the following statements about making decisions. Complete
   the sentences with the words below.

   ambitious   indecisive   independent   responsible   selfish

   1 <u>I guess I'm</u> very _____ because my family always
      comes first. I know that they need my help, and that it's my
      duty to support them.

   2 <u>People say that I'm</u> very _____, because I'm
      determined to follow my dreams and to get to the top in
      whatever I do.

   3 I make sure I get what I want in life, and I'm afraid I don't
      really think about other people at all. <u>I know that I'm</u> very
      _____.

   4 I don't take advice from anyone in particular. I make my
      own decisions. <u>I like to think that I'm</u> very _____.

   5 I hate making choices. <u>I think that I'm</u> really _____.
      I usually just wait to see what happens.

2 **THINK CRITICALLY** Which words in exercise 1 best describe Sala,
   Cham, and Sala's Gran? Discuss with a partner. Give reasons.

   I think that Sala / Cham / Sala's Gran is very … because …

3 How would you describe yourself? Use the words and <u>underlined</u>
   phrases from exercise 1, and describe yourself to your partner,
   giving reasons. If your partner knows you, they can agree /
   disagree, using the following phrases:

   I'm not sure.   *In my opinion, …*
   I think / feel (that)…   *I agree / don't agree.*

1   Read this advertisement for a virtual reality experience.

VIRTUAL DRIVER

A new and exciting virtual reality driving course for anyone over the age of twelve!

Learn to drive a car in complete safety, and to use all the controls with confidence. Unlike with normal driving lessons, *VIRTUAL DRIVER* lets you:

- use the car's controls with confidence.
- understand and remember important road signs.
- learn how to drive safely on all types of roads, including freeways.

....

Things you can only do with *VIRTUAL DRIVER*:

- Experience a huge range of challenging situations without the real dangers of the road.
- Choose the car you drive, or try several different ones!
- Repeat each driving lesson as many times as you wish.

....

With a course of 20 one-hour lessons priced at just $400, *VIRTUAL DRIVER* offers you the cheapest and quickest way of learning the basic driving skills.

Get your free 10-minute trial – visit our website TODAY!

www.virtualdriveroffer.com

* Note that in addition to using the Virtual Driver simulator, you must complete training in a real car, on real roads, in order to pass your National Driver's Test.

2 Answer the questions about the advertisement.

1 What is the name of the experience?

2 What does the company use virtual reality for?

3 Who is the experience for?

4 What is different about this particular experience?

5 How much does it cost?

6 What special offer is given on the website?

7 What important information do you need to know?

3 **COLLABORATE** Work with a partner. Think of a different experience that could use virtual reality. Then think of answers to the questions in exercise 2 for your experience.

4 **CREATE** With your partner, write an advertisement for the experience that you are going to offer. Remember to say how your service is different, who it is for, and how much it costs.

5 **COMMUNICATE** Work in groups. Look at all the advertisements and discuss them. Then vote for the best or most useful virtual reality experience.

If you liked this Bookworm, why not try...

Do Androids Dream of Electric Sheep?

STAGE 5

Philip K. Dick

San Francisco lies under a cloud of radioactive dust. People live in half-deserted buildings, and keep electric animals as pets because many real animals have died. Most people emigrate to Mars, unless they have a job to do on Earth – like Rick Deckard, android killer for the police and owner of an electric sheep. This week, he has to find and kill six androids which have escaped from Mars. They're machines, but they look and sound and think like humans.

The movie *Blade Runner* was based on this famous novel.

I, Robot – Short Stories

STAGE 5

Isaac Asimov

A human being is a soft, weak creature. It needs constant supplies of air, water, and food; it has to spend a third of its life asleep; and it can't work if the temperature is too hot or too cold.

But a robot is made of strong metal. It uses electrical energy directly, never sleeps, and can work in any temperature. It is stronger, more efficient, and sometimes more human than human beings.

Isaac Asimov's short stories give us an unforgettable and terrifying vision of the future.
